ALUN LEWIS (1915–44) was born in Aberdare, South Wales, the son of a schoolmaster. From Cowbridge Grammar School he won a scholarship to the University of Wales at Aberystwyth, gaining a first-class degree in history and in 1935 taking up a research studentship at Manchester University. He returned to Aberystwyth to train as a teacher, working at a secondary school in Pengam and periodically for the WEA and the Left Book Club. In 1939 he met Gweno Ellis, a fellow teacher: they married in 1941, by which time, in spite of his pacifism, Lewis had joined the Royal Engineers. In 1941 he was commissioned and assigned to the South Wales Borderers. He trained at various English military camps before being posted in October 1942 to India. His battalion saw action against the Japanese in Burma, and Lewis died there, near Bawli Bazar, on 5 March 1944.

Lewis's poems were first published while he was a student and in the late 1930s his poetry and short stories attracted critical acclaim when they appeared in journals and magazines. A first book of poems, *Raiders' Dawn*, was published in 1942 and a collection of stories, *The Last Inspection*, in 1943. His reputation as a poet was confirmed by the posthumous publication of *Ha! Ha! Among the Trumpets* (1945). Other books of his writing include *Letters from India* (1946), *In the Green Tree* (1948), *Alun Lewis: A Miscellany of His Writings* (1982), and *Inwards Where All the Battle Is* (1997). Selections of his poetry appeared in 1966 (edited by Ian Hamilton), 1981 (edited by Jeremy Hooker & Gweno Lewis), and 1994 (edited by Cary Archard). A biography by John Pikoulis was published by Poetry Wales Press in 1984.

FREDA AYKROYD (1910–2005) was born in Shropshire, but spent much of her life abroad. In 1930 she married the distinguished nutritionist Wallace Aykroyd and moved with him to Coonoor, South India, where he took up the post of director of the Nutrition Research Laboratories. As well as broadcasting for All India Radio, Freda made the Aykroyds' house in the Nilgiri Hills into a peaceful refuge for convalescent British servicemen. Alun Lewis first visited in 1943, eight months before his death. From an early age Freda wrote poems, novels and stories; some of her stories appeared in *English Story* during the 1940s. Her memoir of Alun Lewis was written in her seventies, after her retirement to Woodstock in Oxfordshire. She is survived by her son and two daughters.

ALUN LEWIS

A Cypress Walk
Letters to 'Frieda'

with a memoir by Freda Aykroyd

ENITHARMON PRESS

First published in 2006
by Enitharmon Press
26B Caversham Road
London NW5 2DU

www.enitharmon.co.uk

Distributed in the UK by
Central Books
99 Wallis Road
London E9 5LN

Distributed in the USA and Canada
by Dufour Editions Inc.
PO Box 7, Chester Springs
PA 19425, USA

ISBN 1 904634 30 3 (hardback)

Enitharmon Press gratefully acknowledges the financial support of
the Welsh Books Council and Arts Council England, London.

British Library Cataloguing-in-Publication Data.
A catalogue record for this book is available
from the British Library.

Designed and typeset by Libanus Press
and printed in England by
Cromwell Press Ltd

Acknowledgements

I wish to thank my children Peter, Gillian and Juliet for encouraging me to write the preface to these letters and to publish them as a dimension necessary to an understanding of the poet and his later poems, letters and journals.

I am grateful to the many people who have written suggesting various interpretations of his writings, which I have quoted in articles.

I would also like to thank Daphne Dorman for her sympathetic understanding and her skilful typing of the manuscript.

FREDA AYKROYD

In preparing my mother's memoir and the Lewis letters for publication, I have been enthusiastically helped by Timothy Rogers and Colin Harris at The Bodleian Library, University of Oxford, which has the original papers in its collection*, and by Thea and Olivia Lacey. Thanks are due to Gweno Lewis for her permission to publish the letters and poems, and to Seren, publishers of Alun Lewis's *Collected Poems*.

JULIET AYKROYD

*The letters and poems illustrated in the text have the following Bodleian reference numbers: MS. Eng. c. 2012, fols. 11v, 12r detail, 21v detail, 47r, 75r detail, 98r, 103v detail; MS. Eng. c. 6074, fol. 10r.

Oh youth-charmed hours, that made an avenue
Of fountains playing on us to love's full view,
A cypress walk to some romantic grave –
Waking, how false in outline and in hue
We find the dreams that flickered on our cave:
Only your fire, which cast them, still seems true.

C. Day Lewis, 'O Dreams, O Destinations'

. . . The wild beast in the cave
Is all our pride; and will not be
Again until the world's blind travail
Breaks in crimson flower from the tree

I am, in Thee.

Alun Lewis, 'A Fragment'

Alun Lewis at Highfield, photographed by Freda Aykroyd (see also page 57)

Remembering Alun Lewis

While Alun Lewis could not write the poems which were stifled in him because of the pressures of war and his loyalty to his wife Gweno, he wrote countless letters to his family and friends in what I feel was a faith-keeping act, in some half-perceived sense a bequest. The letters in this book, written in the last year of his life and perhaps the most self-revealing of any he wrote, show the humanity which stirred him to compassion or anger, his invincible integrity, his longing for creative freedom, and his deepest conception of the true meaning of love. They complete an incomplete understanding of him and will, I hope, help to piece together partly withheld aspects of this remarkable poet.

Coonoor, where I lived with my husband Wallace and our daughter Gilly and where Alun Lewis came on sick leave, was eight thousand feet above sea level in the Nilgiri Hills above Madras in India. These hills are amongst the oldest in the world. Exotic jungle covers their lower slopes. The train chugging up from the plains below passed through it: through Flame-of-the-Forest, brightly-blossomed tulip trees, banana with their huge silky leaves, teak and – hanging like ropes amongst them – curious trailing strands from hidden trees. A high waterfall falling into a deep pool added to the steamy moisture of the air as the train struggled up the steep incline. With each mile accomplished the air grew cooler and clearer until, stepping out of the train in Coonoor, one shivered with a sudden sweet cold.

The quality of the air at that great height is difficult to describe. It caused an excitement, an ecstatic appreciation of life. It was clear

and thin as crystal, sparkling as though the sun were young and had
risen for the first time. It intoxicated one. The colour of the flowers
in the light of the early mornings, before the heat haze softened and
suffused it, was always a lovely salutation to the day. I often came
from my bed into the quickening dawn to watch the garden emerge
and feel the purity and exhilaration of the light and the mountain
air as the sun dispelled the velvet dark of the Indian night.

The train would stop at Coonoor but the ghat road continued on
through Wellington, the military cantonment, past woodland, scat-
tered bungalows and upper grassland until it reached Ootacamund.

Ooty was then not much more than a large village with a bazaar
and Government House to which the Governor and his entourage
would come during the hot weather to escape the heat of Madras.
The British had built a club, an impressive Georgian building, on an
outer hillside. Bungalows with beautiful gardens and lawns were
dotted about the hills. They belonged mainly to British families,

a few wealthy Eurasians and, sparsely, Indians. The gardens of Ootacamund were spoken of nostalgically by the British stationed in other parts of India. Everything grew in them: tropical plants and flowers beside every kind of English garden flower or shrub. A library stocked with surprisingly good books, a Protestant church and a nursing home stamped indelibly upon this Indian village the British way of life. The church was set in the usual sad cemetery where little graves testified to the many child deaths, others to the women who died in bearing them. Soldiers up from the plains dying of malaria or dysentery, or – far back – of wounds, lay here under crumbling headstones on which were inscribed, still visibly, touching tributes to their memory.

The Ooty Downs lay beyond the town: wild rolling hills where panthers trod and jackals howled and the mysterious ancient tribe of Todas built their huts, few and far between, before which they would stand white-clad, watching curiously the occasional fisherman pass by carrying his tackle and wearing his topi. For a river, trout-laden and clear as glass, coursed through the valleys of these Downs. On the hilltops grew sholas, or coppices. In the crooks of their branches orchids flourished in amazing variety and beauty, and on the Downs themselves every ten years, it was said, strobilanthus – a flower of breathtaking blue – made pools of colour in the wind-driven grass. The river ran into a lake, Malmund, beside which the fisherman would picnic and his dog run wild with excitement after the rabbits and jackal or start up an occasional snake.

Coonoor, eleven miles down the ghat road from Ooty, was a small village with the usual bazaar, two shops, post-office, Indian stalls, a Protestant church, a modest hotel and an insignificant club. Wallace's nutrition laboratories were housed in the domed Pasteur Institute whose original purpose was the making of anti-rabies serum.

A small park spread beyond Coonoor. In it grew many of the

jungle trees and a stream ran its peaceful course through rides lit by dappled sunlight. Very few people, surprisingly, seemed to visit this quiet place: an occasional walker would pass along its mossy paths, or a car drive along its wider ways to our house, Highfield, whose gardens touched its outer border. It seemed always to be dreaming undisturbed, its beautiful trees stirred only by the breeze or by birds, some as exotic as the trees themselves. The silence was broken by their song. Alun's poem 'Wood Song' evokes this:

Wood Song

The pine trees cast their needles softly
Darling for your gipsy bed
And the tall blue saplings swaying
Whisper more than can be said.

Piteously the world is happening
Beyond this cool stockade of trees
Enduring passions penetrate
These quiet rides with agonies
That love can never consummate.

And we must go because we love
Beyond ourselves, beyond these trees
That sway above your golden head
Till wind and war and sky and dove
Become again the murmur of your breath
And your body the white shew-bread.

Highfield itself was a large house, Colonial-Georgian, with white columns edging a deep veranda and supporting lacy balconies which ran around the upper floor. Lawns surrounded it and on their

border clustered the trees of the gladed woodland park: jacaranda, mimosa, bougainvillaea, eucalyptus and tree ferns – ferns growing like trees six feet high. The garden was terraced, and it was a sudden delight to come upon it when approaching up the steep drive through the woodlands: the balconied house and the lawns drifting into view, the vivid beds and borders of flowers and a fountain which played in a pool outside the long drawing-room windows. Flowers grew around it and a tree fern spread its fronds above its own reflection.

It was to this house that Alun Lewis came on sick leave on 25 July 1943, and it was in this garden that later I waited each morning for the postman to bring his letters. When in camp he remained without sleep while he wrote through the night; on manoeuvres he wrote under the stars by the light of a hurricane lamp, or sometimes he wrote from a rattling Indian train travelling to where the war so secretly took him. Though desperately overworked, exhausted and often ill, he allowed nothing to reduce the long night hours of writing. Sometimes the postman would bring two letters, sometimes they would contain a poem. I would open them quickly to read that he was not ill, that he had received my letters. For it was through these letters that we gradually became aware of the sameness we shared. I found myself writing to him at all times of the day.

Wallace had been called to attend a conference in America. He was a doctor, a nutrition scientist working for the Government of India (British) as Director of the Nutrition Research Laboratories in the Pasteur Institute in Coonoor. I was busy with various wartime commitments: I helped to run a canteen for the troops, collected clothes from the wives of officers in the regiment then stationed in Wellington or the wives of members of the Indian Civil Service, and sold them to the less fortunate, sending the money to the 'War Fund'. We also kept open house for nurses or soldiers on leave or sick leave.

The drafting of civilians in Britain into the army brought a new kind of officer to India. Most of them were refreshingly different from the regular army who seemed of necessity to be cut to a same pattern. The new stimulus such people provided lessened the restlessness induced by the bell-jar existence which living in India forced upon English women. I had often to fight against a very real melancholy and feeling of waste, for in India domestic routine was handed over to the servants (twelve in my case) who, except for the bearer, cook and chauffeur, seemed to move about in the background of one's life. Deprived of even domestic chores, the lassitude which affected many seemed to sap any vital energy I had. I wrote book reviews for the *Calcutta Statesman* and the *Madras Mail*, an occasional short story, painted a little and occupied myself with the life of our daughter Gilly, about whom I felt a constant fear, for she was frequently ill.

I escaped from this restless discontent by playing squash, golf, bridge: hunted and danced – dancing being in the 1930s as much part of social life as a pre-lunch drink in a pub is today. I longed to have more children but none came. We had left our son Peter, aged seven, in a private school in England thinking we would finally return from India at the end of the year. However, the war broke out in the autumn and he was in due course evacuated to Canada. I grieved desperately at this loss. For many years I had consulted doctors in the Nilgiris and in Madras but remained frustrated and disappointed. Soon after Alun left Coonoor my doctor, who had patiently encouraged me for so long, telephoned to say that Dr Somerville, a surgeon of some repute, was to visit Ooty, and suggested I should consult him. With a certain tired reluctance I did so and he performed what seemed at the time an unnecessary exploratory laparotomy. I recovered quickly, but it was to this operation that Alun, puzzled and concerned, referred in his letters.

One of the officers who came to stay at Highfield on leave was Richard Mills. Before being drafted into the army he had been at the University College of Wales in Aberystwyth with Alun Lewis, with whom he had formed a close friendship. He had a passionate love of literature and became the perfect audience for Alun, who would read his poems to him, inviting his opinion.

Dick talked of his friend Alun Lewis, showed me Alun's first book of poems, *Raiders' Dawn*, and because he loved Highfield asked if he could come again on his next leave, bringing Alun with him. In the event Alun was refused leave so Dick came up without him. In due course a regretful letter came from Alun, the first in this collection – a somewhat strained attempt to introduce himself. Sometime after Dick had gone I received a telegram: 'May get leave Thursday. Can I come and see you arriving Saturday. Will wire when definite. Alun Lewis.' No further telegram came and I forgot about this possible visit. Then one morning, unexpectedly and typically, Alun himself arrived.

The Map [unpublished]

Across the battles and famine areas,
I wrote your name upon the map
And then I laid the map away
Because the map became the world
And every road contained a death
And I was willing that the world
Should have its pleasure with my breath.
I laughed to keep my spirits up
Having put away the map
And fought my way into the world.

I lay in sickness in the world
And heard that you were lying sick
I dreamed in sickness of the map
The battles and the famines and your name
But you became another world
Unapproachable in space
I did not know your silken lap
Nor your animated face.

And then your name became yourself
And the world became your name
And you yourself were standing there
Among the teacups and the shame.
My darkness was a fillet for your hair.

And when you lay within my arms
The human passion in me cried
With the voice of every man
Who had that wound within his side

And knew the beauty of the world
And hated that by which he died.

But loveliness is no man's bride.

Your name is mixed with battles on the map
And I can lie no longer by your side
Because the world has laid away the map,
And I can never lay away the world.

Though much has faded from my memory his arrival stays as vivid
as lightning. I was helping Gilly to arrange her dolls and their furniture in a dolls' house I had had made for her by the local carpenter,
when Mari (grandly and inappropriately named 'the Butler') came
up to the balcony to say an officer sahib had arrived. Sighing a little,
wondering which of my list of visitors it could be, I told Mari to
bring him up. Suddenly he was standing in the doorway.

Beloved when we stood
And saw each other standing there
I did not know that all
The ordinary days
Had fallen from the earth.*

I knew at once who he was. He was wiry-looking, dark and 'foreign'
as are many of the Welsh valley men, and there was a frailty about
him, a look of not belonging in all this horror and mess of war, in
his white face and his fine high forehead. He had been in hospital
with a broken jaw and dysentery. He looked tired and there was
a curious dreaming contemplation in his eyes as he looked at me.
I saw that he was very shy. Still kneeling, with a toy in my hand,

* 'The House', unpublished poem

I looked up at him. Neither spoke – some recognition seemed to replace words. The colour rose in my face as I got up slowly.

'Alun?' I said.

He sighed as he answered, in a voice so low that it was almost inaudible: 'Yes. I'm sorry I didn't send a telegram – it was too late, you see. I caught the first train as soon as my leave came through.' He spoke always in this low voice with its soft Welsh intonation.

'This is Gilly,' I said.

He came out from the doorway onto the verandah, put his hand on Gilly's head, pushing it back a little, and looked into her face.

'Gilly,' he said, and smiled.

From that moment Gilly became his slave. We went down to tea on the lawn and I remember how she put her hand into his – an unusual gesture for she was a shy child. In the short time he was at Highfield he grew to love her as he did all children.

Before I knew that Alun would be with me I had accepted an invitation to a dinner party that night which was to include a dance at the Wellington Club. I telephoned Gloria, the hostess, suggesting I should bring Alun with me.

Alun was an efficient and intelligent officer who worked at his regimental duties with desperate intensity, careless of his own health. He was committed to these duties – as he was to the troops – by a tremendous sense of responsibility, although he hated the war and the preparation for it. Yet on occasion he showed a vagueness, an almost childish helplessness. A small incident that first evening made me aware of this. As Wallace was away Gloria had asked another guest, a young subaltern, to fetch me.

I was waiting for Alun in the drawing-room, dressed in evening dress as was then usual on such occasions, when he came through the door from his bedroom. He was holding the top of his khaki trousers together, smiling with the curious mixture of shyness and composure I learned to know in him.

'A pin?' he asked in his soft voice.

I went to look for a safety-pin and returned to the drawing room to find the subaltern (whom I greeted absently) staring surprised at the half-dressed officer. I have the vividest memory of the unself-conscious sharing of the small task with Alun: his bowed head as he held the band, my fingers aware of the warm flesh beneath his khaki shirt and above all the sense of an old intimacy, one which asked of him no apology, no light conversational comment from me. The presence of the other young man seemed irrelevant – we hardly noticed him. Alun wrote later:

> The first evening when someone called to take you (me thrown in) to Gloria's dinner party, I remember the spontaneous unquestioning feeling I had that the man who called was from outside and that it had happened to us & we didn't belong except to each other. A marvellous feeling of blood relationship, not then of a lover but of a brother (not only a brother): and I'll always have that, though there are so many imponderable antagonistic forces and so many weaknesses in me that prevent & prevent.

This incident, so clear in my memory, drew us together in a bond (light at that moment) which endured until his death, a bond which resisted the agonies and bewilderments which grew in him over the coming year. The absence of self-consciousness in the innocent task of pinning his trousers' band was an indication of something we grew to recognise as we exchanged our constant letters: a sibling-like closeness, an instinctive and protective understanding. 'I have this new feeling always that I can ask of you anything I can ask of myself: that if there is in me either desire or willingness or, these being absent, pure passive faith in what comes to pass, then it is also in you.' Through our letters we discovered to our delight that we shared strong similarities.

Tree fern and fountain in the garden at Highfield

'Do you like being each other?' 'It *is* uncanny,' he wrote, 'how we seem to think the same things, quite independently. I don't think them because you are thinking them. It isn't telepathic. It's because we are in the same place in eternity; our alonenesses are identical, our spirits have the same calluses and same ferocities, and the same vulnerable sides. I rarely feel that I am thinking the same things as you, though sometimes I do. But generally I think in the heart of a wide and stony aloneness and I simply observe that you also thought just that just then. And I don't understand why it should be like that . . .' And later: '. . . you are so uncannily close to me in moods & *times* of feeling . . .' '. . . God, this uncanny understanding – so close that it becomes invisible, immanent, unnecessary.'

We shared a melancholy. In me it was spasmodic and unguessed at by others who saw me, I think, as humorous. (In a letter to Dick Mills, Alun wrote: '. . . she has a deep complex due to the conviction that she was unloved as a child. It is too late to change her now but it gives her some of her wildness and freedom.' Perhaps this was true.) In him melancholy was emphasised by depression, the onslaught of which illness he dreaded and could not fend off, and which when it occurred drove him to the outermost extremes of despair. His unpublished poem 'Love' dedicated 'NOT to Frieda, but to TIME', intimates these feelings:

> The heart compels
> And I have cause to fear
> The wounds and disasters
> When love is near.
>
> Love has done with peace.
> Love is at war.
> Her harsh gyrating engines
> Thunder afar.
>
> . . . With shrinking and longing
> Love tears me asunder.
>
> Unbearable ecstasy, how can I answer
> Possessed with your splendour, having no choice,
> That other bitter agony,
> That other broken voice?
> Am I not cruel, as you are,
> So to rejoice?

Alun and I shared a profound need for what he called freedom – a word which when used by him encompassed much more than its specific meaning. It was one of two contradictory needs which deeply affected his life: a longing for an unfettered, independent existence which would free him to live in his own lonely, often mystic world where he could fulfil his creative self. 'I've always refused to submit to a rule . . . I've clung as far as possible to the freedom that does not decide and scarcely has an opinion, that suddenly acts from an overpowering conviction that appears to be simple intuition, and acts always *in* the situation, and not according to the rules that one applies to the situation.' 'Many things may happen to us, but nothing that can trap and destroy the – the what? The freedom of heaven & earth & time. Isn't that what we apprehended? I know how I lose & fail back into time & the impotence of time: but I don't think these small stumblings & wounds & disasters in time can really matter much one way or the other to that great freedom that one can only leave alone. Because it IS. That's all. It IS.'

Ian Hamilton, in his biographical introduction to *Alun Lewis: Selected Poetry and Prose* (George Allen & Unwin, 1966), describes Alun's longing for freedom as a need to follow the solitary routes of the imagination. This is partly true, for isolation is the primary instinct of the poet. But there was also a longing, unique to himself, for isolation in some dream world, unknown but longed for: '. . . the dark imagination that would pierce infinite night.' 'I want to break out of it like a clown through a paper hoop. Break out of this into that – will it be the same each side like a clown's hoop, or amazingly different, like the chrysalid & the butterfly?'

Before he came to India he experienced what he called a vision in which he became aware of a dream world of great beauty and solitary peace which called to him, promising him fulfilment in the writing of 'wonderful poetry'. He had been obsessed with the skeleton of a poem, mysterious, obscure – one feels its meaning is obscure to himself. He wrote:

Those words came out of me and they came up into me . . . gradually in about three days I came to see a vision . . . I've been nothing but the images which those words, repeating themselves day and night in my mind, evoked. Beautiful ice-cold death images of perfect poetry. 'Can't you see? Can't you SEE?' they were saying – and I could see high upland pastures with white milky waters falling in foam-fans over the green rocks. And those pastures and those waters falling have been everything. On and on, up and on into the horizon of hills and sky-lines and clean black flow of rock against a dawn rain red sky soft as snow. But a silent land. 'Can't you see?' the words said. 'Alone – come alone. This is the home of the soul, its freedom to wander, alone and released – released from the body and the situation. A spirit world.' I grew lonelier and more blessed, more rapt than I have ever been. And I thought, I can write wonderful poetry now I have the way to poetry – the vision.*

His dream world and the lonely pursuit of self-fulfilment extended into what he called his ideal of love:

. . . but the *real* music is in being thrillingly & sensitively aware of the separateness of the other one with whom you share love and who is in your arms or in bed with you or five thousand miles away from you. But always you are aware that the beloved is complete, *herself*, & life that just by being itself strikes incessant music out of the silences. And when you do come together, then, God! what music is audible, drowns you, yet is only just audible, beautiful. That's the way I want to love, not this begging and this leaning, but a calm independent love that endures absence and rejoices in meeting and doesn't destroy or crimp or cripple.

This ideal of love, where lovers part and come together over the miles or years to meet in sublime fulfilment, he composed into an

---

* The words that inspired this vision, which seemed to come from some mysterious source, were written down as a poem. (*Raiders' Dawn*, George Allen and Unwin, 1942). They were never reworked though the publishers suggested they should be. He called the poem 'Peace': 'I can only say it grew into that, because (the vision became) a dream of peace, such peace. So I gave it that name.'

allegory of our being two beasts; it was very dear to him and he wrote about it with a curious almost secret comprehension: '. . . the yellow-eyed proud soft-moving beasts that go their own way and in some clearing in the jungle sometimes come upon each other and become thereby sublime.' [. . .] 'It's the only really fundamental truth we mean. It's the only miracle over which we have no control.' He wrote a draft poem containing it:

The Transmigration of Love

There was the sea moving against the seawall along a
                                     curving league
And the pleasure parks where time is killed by playboys
                                     and the more
Fresh-air sort of whores,
And two loving each other, linked in the spying crowd,
Their bodies radiating and fulfilling each other from
                                     a window
To which a chokra child brought lotus every day.

When the world entered the minds of these lovers
It more nearly attained its peaceful potential,
And ugliness achieved its long-refused transcendence
Over suffering as authentic as the strata of mountains.

Naked within their love in a bed in a window
They made the end an image of their love.
And the end was death,
Not for them only, but all the time for someone
In a bomb or bullet, malaria, cholera, sunstroke;
And the end for these two lovers began a way back in
                                     the beginning,

In the perception of life perhaps of a child of seven
Seeing a baby born or a new kind of grasshopper,
And growing through the loneliness of youth,
The uniqueness that is like a virginity in youth,
Into a wilder, deeper, more general prevision –

Envisaging a slim spaced forest, a gladed darkness
Fretted with fireflies and the touch
Of long cool grasses each on each
And through the scrub the instinctive trails and spoors,
The opaque yielding awareness of animals,
Wild beasts, smooth and evasive, tawny-eyed complete creatures –

And in that deep familiar darkness the loving elements conjoined
In the endlessly desired mutation of decay and generation.

Later he used the allegory in a short poem:

> ### A Fragment
>
> Where aloneness fiercely
> Trumpets the unsounded night
> And the silence surges higher
> Than hands or seas or mountains' height
>
> I the deep shaft sinking
> Through the quivering Unknown
> Feel your anguish beat its answer
> As you grow round me, flesh and bone.
>
> The wild beast in the cave
> Is all our pride; and will not be

Again until the world's blind travail
Breaks in crimson flower from the tree

I am, in Thee.

The second need, so vital to him and in curious contradiction to his longing for freedom, was for the reassurance of the love of his family and of Gweno – 'The warm ones about us', 'Those to whom we owe ourselves . . . those who shaped us.' He responded to their love with a love of equal intensity.

He was haunted by death, as many depressives are. It was always in his mind: he spoke about it, wrote about it – sometimes with loathing, at other times with something like joy: 'I *do* think of death a great deal, and I think life and human relationships have grown more & more precious & warm and urgent to me because of this thought at the back of everything.'

If we identify the thoughts of the dying Christ in Alun's poem 'The Crucifixion' with those of Alun himself, we find echoes of his two great needs as well as of death:

. . . Foreseeing a time when the body and all its injunctions
And *life* and *people** and all their persistent demands
Would desist . . .

. . . And this surrender of self to a greater statement
Has been desired by many more humble than he.
But when it came, was it other than he had imagined?
Breaking his Self up, convulsing his Father in pain?
His will prevented by every throbbing stigma,
The pangs that puffed and strained his stomach wall,

* his emphases

26

The utter weariness that bowed his head,
Taught him perhaps that more hung on the presence
Of all the natural preoccupations
Duties, emotions, daily obligations
Affections and responses than he'd guessed.
They'd grown a burden to him, but as a mother
Is burdened by her child's head when her breasts
Are thin and milkless . . .

The 'body and all its injunctions/And *life* and *people* and all their persistent demands' – these had become a burden to him yet he accepted them through love: a love which threatened to drain the life-giving substance from him – his creative self.

On the evening of his arrival, after I had pinned together the waistband of his trousers, we were driven by the neglected subaltern to Wellington where Gloria's bungalow stood on a hill above the club. We were late in arriving and found her living-room filled with officers and their wives or girl friends. She was not pleased: we had kept her from taking her guests into dinner and I had upset her table plan by bringing Alun. She looked at him critically as I introduced them, obviously recognising in his demeanour an alien in their midst.

'*Come* on Freda. No time for drinks – if we're ever to get to this miserable dance.'

'We'd love a quick drink.'

'Sorry – no time.'

As we went in to dinner the Colonel put his hand upon my arm. 'Bad luck, Freda,' he said, adding, no doubt to smooth my ruffled feathers, 'You look very slinky in that dress.' He was a kindly man, who had become a close friend of Wallace and me. He was killed in Burma a few months later, as were two other men at that dinner party. One of them went into Burma and was quite simply never heard of again: he left behind four young children and the nicest wife in the regiment.

I was at the opposite end of the dinner table from Alun and watched nervously for fear of any embarrassment to him, his shyness and his Welsh tones seeming a hazard. But he was sitting next to the wife soon to be widowed, talking seriously, his beautiful face and dark head attracting more than one glance from others. He, too, was to die – within a year. I could have no knowledge of it, but knew only the suppressed fear shared by everyone and symbolised by the khaki uniform worn by the men around the table. After dinner we were hustled into various cars.

'Freda, you come with us,' Gloria said.

'And Alun?'

'Oh Alun,' she said, a little weary, a little patronising.

As we were driven down the ghat road huge stars shone almost musically in the Indian night sky, and the dark was filled with sound: distant wailing music from the bazaar, a jackal's howl, the creaking of a bullock cart as it ground up the hill, while in the car laughter and tipsy talk as Alun and I sat silent. We arrived late at the dance, the band playing 'Top Hat' and uniformed officers dancing with women who wore slightly out-of-date dresses, while club servants moved about barefooted with trays of drinks.

I can remember only the end of that evening. I was sitting on a fire-seat before the fire; an officer was deeply asleep with a glass of whisky beside him, Gloria was describing the dress she was to wear for her coming wedding, and Alun was silent in his chair. I was tired and glanced at him, hoping to go home. He looked exhausted as he listened dreamily to Gloria, nodding his head and clearly unaware of what she was saying. She fell silent and I called to Alun.

He describes in a letter how he rose from his chair and came to sit beside me, putting his arm along my shoulders and his face in my hair: how then he *knew* ('I can't write that word "knew" strongly enough') that he loved me. I did not realise this, only that he had come so naturally into this gentle embrace. The band was now playing 'Goodnight Ladies' and, feeling sad and somehow bereft as I always did when a dance ended, I asked the patient subaltern if he would drive us home to Highfield. Refusing to come in, he drove away while Alun and I stood in the fern-filled portico of the house. Alun put his arms around me and began to talk. I had no idea what he was saying for his voice was almost a whisper; only an occasional word was audible. I never asked him later what he had been saying that night as we stood in the moonlight amongst the ferns.

The next morning and each day after that we wandered in the woods where Alun said moles lay ('In mole-blue indolence the sun/ Plays idly on the stagnant pool' is the first line of 'The Jungle'), watching the stream busily flowing over the pebbles and tenderly embracing beneath the trees. We sat in the garden and read, sometimes to each other, listened to music on the gramophone which Mari had brought out onto the lawn, talked – endlessly talked – of the past, of ourselves, going deep, sharing each other. And we laughed – for we were happy though life was not really very merry.

How could I help but tremble
Entering your gate
And discovering you there
Standing by the tall blue window
With the sunlight on your hair,
Oh more beautiful than fate.

Yet I did not dissemble
Nor hide myself from you,
But being of soldiers and peasants
Told the endurance of their lives,
And you were the peasant, I the soldier,

But we, because the sky was blue,
Forgot the darkness and the knives.
A word still to be spoken made us tremble.
Life was too elemental to dissemble.*

We pushed the war away as far as we were able, though we were acutely aware of it, as we were aware that this love was wounding to the other loves to which we were committed. But Wallace and Gweno were thousands of miles away, we were young, alone in a paradise high in those ancient Indian mountains, and life pulsed in us, conspiring with all the many delights of the mind which we shared, together with the youthful beauty each saw in the other, to draw us unresisting into the closed circle of love. It was an idyll, romantic yet scrupulous, for no word of love was spoken during those few charmed days – 'A word yet to be spoken made us tremble.' In the draft of a poem which appears in radically different form in his *Collected Poems* ('Beloved Beware'), Alun wrote of this time:

> Love is never born complete
> But needs time to dry
> Its wings born of water
> Like the dragonfly.
>
> Is there time or room to grow?
> Beloved, beware,
> Before you say 'let it be so'
> Love is already there.
>
> . . . If you lose too much
> By loving me, forswear
> All I secreted for you,

* Unrevised unpublished poem

30

Beloved, beware,
When emotion burns the soul
Love is already there.

I wrote differently – though I did not show him my poems at the time but only when he asked me later to send them to him in camp:

The Exquisite Moment

This is the moment of happiness:
Now when the heart knows surely
This new love given purely –
Love in its loveliness.

When only the heart stirs,
Not brain nor blood nor any sensual need;
Now before these, urgent, plead
Reassurance or fulfilment yet again.

And before the eager telling,
The whispered word which is too loud
For this quiet certainty and proud
Joy in my young heart welling.

After some days I began to think unhappily of Wallace. I wanted to be alone to welcome him when he came back. I told Alun this and he understood. I suggested that he should go up to Ooty to an officers' rest home, Ratantata, for a few days. Although we would part reluctantly, I think in some sense he was glad of this suggestion, for though he did not tell me so, he felt love-inspired poems forming in him and longed to give them (as he once wrote) hospitality.

So Wallace returned and I told him of Alun's visit, of the poet he was, of his love for Gilly and hers for him – but I did not tell him of the unexpressed romantic love which had sprung up between us.

In Ooty Alun hired a bicycle and rode out on to the wild and beautiful downs. He sat by the great river, struggling to give substance to the new poems, and paced his bedroom all night seeking words in desperate creative urgency. The poems he brought back to me are lovely lyrical ones, filled with sadness and longing. In a letter he describes how when he was at the Intelligence School in Karachi he showed these poems to a friend he liked and admired. The friend, reading them as they sat in a cheap Chinese restaurant, decided that they were 'facile'. Alun was devastated by this. He wrote to me: 'He said facile. It hurt like hell & bloody hell . . . It *wasn't* facile, Christ it wasn't. Michael, why did you say that?' He never after this regarded these poems with true appreciation and he grieved the more when new poems did not come. I have blamed myself for not writing to point out to him that those to whom one dares to show one's creative treasures often feel that some response is expected, and are compelled to offer one, however ignorant.

In Coonoor Wallace talked of the conference in Hot Springs. He was excited and stimulated by it and his part in it, and I loved him and was as always proud of him.

After several days Alun returned from Ooty. His return is another luminous memory. It was as unexpected as his first arrival at Highfield. We had not set a date for it nor had he telephoned. Typically he had acted upon a sudden impulse. He had taken the ramshackle bus full of poor people and their chattels. He carried in his hand the poems he had written and as he approached through the trees, shunning the usual path, he waved to me as I stood by chance at the long window. I did not know, of course, what the sheaf of papers in his hand was but I was touched suddenly by his approach as he weaved his way through the trees with an air of suppressed excitement, like a boy held in check though longing to race ahead. This boyishness was a great part of the impression he made; it combined oddly with the intellectual power, the genius his work displayed. There was always this impression of suppressed emotion in him. However still or thoughtful, whether talking or laughing, there was this intensity, a suggestion of waiting, which communicated itself however remote he remained, however near he came. Now, stepping into the room, he kissed me, looked at me for a long moment then, waving the sheaf of papers, 'Shall I?' he asked and I nodded. He sat down and began to read the beautiful lyrical poems, sad, all of them, filled with love and longing and haunted by fear of hurt – to Gweno and to us. All he was to feel as that year wore on was expressed in those poems from his heart and from his relentless mind. As I listened, moved to tears, I felt for the first time the threat of pain which had not touched me during the enchanted days when we seemed alone in the world. But he, I saw now, had ached with this realisation from the moment we met when he was, as he put it, struck as though by a sword. The word yet to be spoken was contained in every poem and I knew – what I had surely guessed – that he loved me.

I do not remember the rest of that day, only evenings when he and Wallace talked as I had not heard Wallace talk for a long time – intense, searching arguments, sudden agreement and as sudden disagreement: Wallace the older experienced man with a scientific mind, committed to international politics and welfare; Alun the young soldier and eager Socialist, his politics, though widely applied, impassioned by his experience of the Depression in Wales. Alun wrote in his last letter to Dick Mills of 'all the good things now in jeopardy' if he died (he knew he was to die), amongst them 'Wallace and his labs and his books and our good tough arguments.'

These last days were shadowed by the realisation that they were to be brief and that his return to his camp was imminent. Still we did not speak of love though his poems had changed the happiness we had shared to something more intense. They had made evident what I at least had accepted, whether from fear or loyalty, should remain unsaid. The day before he left we were walking in the woods, sunshine slanting through the trees and the air heavy with the scent of oleander. Neither spoke – there seemed nothing to say; each knew what the other was feeling. Alun stopped beneath a tree and slowly drew me down beside him. He then lay back, his dark hair among the leaves, and very gently took my hand and laid it upon his body so that I felt him move and strengthen beneath my hand. He sighed breathlessly. Then came the bitter failure when his strength left him, his passion faded. He got up, and threw back his head in a proud agony. His face was white. 'Well if that's the way it must be . . .' His voice trembled. I was frantic to lessen the pain, the anguish in his face. 'It will be all right.' I hardly knew what I was saying. 'It will be *all right*.' He then told me fiercely that if it had not been for this he would not have written a word of poetry.

The next morning I came down early knowing that he was to catch the first train down to Mettapalyam. Mari was carrying his suitcase across the drawing-room as I came in and Alun followed him. His newly-laundered khaki jacket, khaki socks pulled up to his knees, the polished shoes and the parted hair bespoke the soldier, waiting for orders or about to give them. His casual clothes were put away in the tightly strapped suitcase together, I felt, with the joy of the past two weeks. He put his arms around me, his head against mine, then stood back, jerking down his jacket. He took my hand and led me out of the room.

Joseph our driver was at the front door with the car and we drove through the woods where so much had happened to us, through Coonoor bazaar to the station. The train was at the platform and at the sight of it I felt the sudden sharp pain of parting. We looked at each other: there was to be no sign of what we were feeling for there were various khaki-clad figures on the platform. Alun kissed me briefly on the cheek and got into the train. I stood watching as he slammed the carriage door and the train collected itself and slowly, squeaking, drew away down the line. I watched until the back of the last carriage grew small in the distance. The world was suddenly empty and silent – even the cries of the tea vendors 'cha, cha!' and the fruit sellers 'orangee, orangee!' had ceased with the departing train. Driving back through the woods the tightness in my throat loosened and tears ran down my face. Gilly was in the garden and I clasped her in my arms. I had come back to where and to whom I belonged and love must accept that. That night I wrote:

The Parting

Last night you wept and your bowed head
Was touching and defenceless as a child's.
Your quiet weeping was my strength –
I stood between you and the world.
But today in the cold and cruel dawn,
Today, uncompromising day, the grey light
Awakened you to your own strength
And left me to my helplessness.
As your fingers fastened buckles deftly,
Efficient and tidy – oh, for what? –
Your lips were firm, I could not see your eyes.
Your khaki jacket rustled stiffly
As you jerked it down behind,
Efficient and clean and ready,
A straw in the wind, a leaf upon the flood.
As you turned to go I saw your eyes
And knew my strength was but despair
And that your own could not prevail.

The garden at Highfield and woods beyond

Some days later I was as so often in the garden in my night-dress having watched dawn break. The flowers were fragrant and their colours bright before the sun took both scent and colour with the growing day. The postman on his early round came up the drive and gave me Alun's first love letter. His poems had told me of the love I knew he felt; their longing and seeming acceptance of sacrifice ('... we must go because we love / Beyond ourselves, beyond these trees ...' '... And your body the white shew-bread') made them sad, their longing ineluctable. But this first love letter seemed to speak secretly, as on that first night amongst the ferns: its singing tone expressing the very essence of love. At last the word was spoken: 'I love you, love you, love you.' The letter is filled with a dreaming happiness: 'My mind rejects all other things as it rejected all things with you except the music and the delight.' '... I have no wish to weep but only to sing and dream.'

Alas, this delight turned all too soon to desperate self-searching and anguished consideration of 'the enormous costs'. His mind 'working in the lowest coal seams' examines, rejects, accepts. 'I know I am involved utterly and entirely in what is happening, and I know that more depends upon it than just life'. In his third letter the painful bewilderment had already begun. It was in nearly every letter until his death. His love was nearly always expressed with an accompanying anguish. 'You spoke very bravely & forwardly in your letter: about . . . the acknowledging over which there is a veil. How or when this will come to pass, we don't know. But it is always coming to pass, always moving towards it. I haven't slept for two nights on this exercise & I've sweated and exerted myself hugely, & yet I'm not tired because of this sleepless longing for the veil to fall off, for the reality to come.' 'I only know that we will have to hang on to *nothing* for long tracts of time, Frieda, and that it is imperishable – *this*.' 'Oh God, it is the very fibre of my being.' He declared that he could never 'unless I die within myself, and I have cause to dread that more than you, deny this love, this burning image of you in me and in the world.' And in one of his last letters he wrote: 'I want you to know I am conscious all the time that a whole life is being thrown away all the time that we deny & are denied each other . . . It makes the rest of living sad.'

Alun had orders to go to the Intelligence School in Karachi when his leave was ended. He stopped for a day in his camp in Kharakvasla near Poona and then continued the six days' train journey to Karachi. It was on this journey that he wrote 'The Way Back', a free exultant poem devoid of the inhibitions and guilt which so exhausted him and filled him with such despair – they were yet to come.

'The Way Back' was first named 'The Return'; the revised title expresses all the passion which the poem conveys. It would not have been possible for a poet newly overwhelmed by love and journeying in a train for six days, withdrawn from the world, not to have written a love poem. But this poem lifts the theme of love out of its romantic setting into something less idyllic: into a mood where romantic nostalgia is joyful, confident, a mood induced by the desire for some cataclysmic force to break up life as it had been, but which had now become something to be 'squandered': a force to 'hurl' him, powerless but free, back to the love which had caused new growth in his now 'green mind', as the rain had brought green growth to the parched earth over which he was travelling.

The Way Back*

Six days and two thousand miles
I have watched the shafted rain
Feminise the burning land,
Cloaking with a green distress
The cerulean and the ochre
Of the season's ruthlessness.

Six days and two thousand miles
I have gone alone
With a green mind and you
Burning in the stubborn bone.

Soldiers quickened by your breath
Feel the sudden spur and rush
Of the life they put away
Lest the war should break and crush
Beauties more profound than death.

I swam within your naked lake
And breasted with exquisite ease

---

* As published in *Collected Poems* (Bridgend: Seren, 1994), pages 127–8. A draft of the poem was incorporated in Lewis's letter of 8 August 1943 (see below, pages 75–6).

The foaming arabesques of joy
And in the sarabande of trees
Of guava and papaya
And crimson blown poinsettia,
The millrace of my blood
Beat against my smile,
And were you answering my smile
Or the millrace of my blood?

But now the iron beasts deploy
And all my effort is my fate
With gladiators and levies
All laconic disciplined men
I pass beyond your golden gate.

And in the hardness of this world
And in the brilliance of this pain
I exult with such a passion
To be squandered, to be hurled,
To be joined to you again.

The poems Alun wrote in Ooty are gentle, filled with longing, their music saddened by a guessed-at pain to come. They are limpid as the dappled sunlight which came through the trees in the woodlands about which he wrote. In contrast 'The Way Back' is vibrant with exotic colour and movement: *poinsettia, guava, papaya*, the trees moving in a *sarabande* – a dignified yet passionate dance. Strange lacquered words – *levies, gladiators* – lift reality into something grander, more magnificent. Officers have become laconic, disciplined men, words which also suggest a dignity above military exercises and the lecture hall, yet an irrevocability. The whole is a poem of intense awareness of the passion newly aroused in him, and his desire to sacrifice all else to it. In an early poem Alun wrote of a woman's 'dark rich love' and this poem embodies these words. As John Pikoulis says in his biography of Alun: ' "The Way Back" . . . expresses a sense of achievement and it comes from the full man in a way none of his other poems do.'

Alun's letter brought my love for him into a reality I had not felt when he was in Coonoor. Then I dreamed romantically, feeling that the unreal war-world in which we lived would last for ever, that some improbable influence would make possible what was impossible. His letters revealed what I already knew to be a mind and imagination overflowing and insatiable; but as time went on I grew aware of something more elusive and profound than the instinctive understanding and concern we had for each other. As I read his letters in the peaceful garden at Highfield, I gained some comprehension of what lies hidden in the dark of the imagination – glimpses of an inescapable beauty, undefined and inexpressible. What there was of the poet in me responded to the poet in him as a lighthouse silently signals its awareness of the flashing of light from its far-distant twin. I think Alun had felt it from the beginning but it was his letters which awakened this recognition in me, and made more true the sense of each being part of the other.

From his earliest letters came the desperate anxiety that we would not meet again and the appeal – though he was at first shy of making it – for me to go to him. 'You will come, Frieda, won't you? Please, please, please.' 'Frieda, come to me. It doesn't matter when . . . but when it happens it will be happening for now and for ever. And Time couldn't alter the truth, but only the when . . . if only you say you'll come when we can . . . let him have his when.' 'I want to meet you so badly, so much I want the comfort of being with you.' I found his pleading heart-breaking. It also frightened me. He seemed so desperate. 'Oh God, Frieda. What is to become of all this? Do you know? I don't.' I was frightened also of my own response to his pleading for, though infidelity seemed unthinkable I yet could not accept that I would never see him again. In me it was a longing, in him a need. He often wrote of a tranquillity he found in me – which surprised me. Was it perhaps a tranquillity in himself? Like most poets he had always sought love. Was it that his restless search for the love he most desired had ceased? ('All I secreted for you', he wrote in the early draft 'Beloved Beware'.) Perhaps the absolute quality of his feeling accounted for much of this. He once wrote that although he had seen me 'with my own eyes' with Wallace and Gilly, he could not think of me as being 'other than my woman – and that is all I can see you as being.' And yet he could write a most beautiful and true interpretation of married love: 'the other love I receive and have given, which so powerfully shaped and directed me . . . You know all this; as you know that these words & feelings are said & felt for ever & alter for ever & one is never the same afterwards as before.' These words applied with an especial truth to my own love for Wallace, for I was not much older than a schoolgirl when we married and he had indeed powerfully shaped and directed me. I felt as Alun did, that 'I would not have imagined that this also would happen which happened to us, nor that we could enter in of ourselves into such liberty and such untrammelled ways.' My love for Alun and my love for Wallace were two different worlds, as were Alun's for Gweno and for me. The dichotomy in Alun drove him to despair. In me it was not a divided love but two loves: one romantic and perfectly fulfilled in Alun's great love for me, the other married love for Wallace intensified by a childhood need – 'My little craft afloat upon your sea,' I once wrote for him.

Yet Alun's pleading tempted me and made me wretched with indecision. Events seemed to decide for me. Before I met Alun I had promised Dick Mills I would when possible visit him in Poona, which was near his camp. Wallace was at this time due to go to Delhi to make his annual report to the Viceroy. I would dearly have loved to go with him but he always preferred to go on his professional travels alone. So I decided to go to Alun. It was a difficult decision to make: I felt as divided in my loyalties as he did, unwilling to betray Wallace and to do what in those days was a very unconventional not to say shocking thing. But I half convinced myself that there was no great culpability in my visiting Dick in Poona as I had promised him, and to go on to nearby Bombay to meet Alun. I tried to make innocent in my mind what was dramatically not so.

The long train journey, lasting two days, was hot and dusty. I felt a nervous excitement. I had not left the Nilgiris since the war began and the landscape of distant mountains and near plains, the haunting scenes which India timelessly presents, enchanted me: a funeral passing slowly down a nearby track with the garlanded corpse lying peaceful on an open bier; monkeys leaping at the windows when the train slowly drew into some small station where the tea-sellers called 'cha, cha' and 'orangee' with their tea-urns on their heads; a horseman galloping down a dry river bed; the paddy fields in which moved quiet figures sad-seeming in the evening light – these scenes, made more vivid by a guilty sense of adventure and a nervous joy at the thought of meeting Alun again, remain in my memory.

Dick met me in Poona. As I stepped down from the train his great bear hug expressed what he felt: delight that his two best-loved friends had met through him and were – as Alun put it – 'no longer Alun and Frieda but us.' It was a naïve and thoughtless joy in Dick, innocently disregarding the pain involved, which both distressed and touched Alun.

Dick took me to the Poona Hotel, a modest but comfortable place. I do not remember anything about Poona itself other than the tarmac drive leading up to the Poona Club, lined with innumerable flower-pots in which grew red cannah lilies. What is unforgettable is my first morning in that little hotel. I awoke, hot under the mosquito net, showered and dressed and was going into the breakfast room when the smell of bacon suddenly induced a great nausea in me. I turned and rushed back to my bedroom where I was sick. There was no mistaking that particular curious nausea – I remembered it: I was pregnant. Dr Somerville's operation – in which I had had little faith – had miraculously achieved what he had intended. Half incredulous, wholly joyful, I sat on the edge of the bed turning what seemed the wonder of it in my mind. Its implications – fear at its effect on Alun – what would he feel? Would my joy hurt him? There was no question of my keeping the truth from him, even temporarily: we were too near for any reservation or secrecy. He would accept it, I decided; he would be as joyful as I was. Of course he would. Although the child would be another imponderable in the situation, it was also part of me whom he loved. So my thoughts ran. I wanted to be with Wallace, to see the surprise and pleasure in his face when I told him. I wanted to be with Alun to share my happiness.

As the train from Poona drew into Bombay station I felt a shyness at the prospect of meeting Alun which I had never felt before. I was about to become his mistress and the role was one I felt entirely unable to assume. I stood on the platform with my suitcase beside me, unhappily uncertain. Alun had said he would meet me there or, if his train was late, at the Taj Mahal Hotel. Suddenly I hated the idea of the Taj Mahal Hotel with its sophisticated luxury and suggestion of illicit liaisons. Then I saw him coming towards me. There was a confidence about him, a sense of authority I had not seen in Coonoor. He took my face in his hands, looked into my eyes and kissed me. Again I felt the new confidence in him: he was the soldier now, not the troubled poet. He lifted the red handkerchief hanging from my pocket and studied its pattern of small giraffes. 'Hel*lo* giraffes,' he said and we laughed; and as he took up my suitcase and led me towards the exit my uncertainty and shyness vanished and the excited joy I had felt on the journey to Poona flooded over me. He was Alun, part of me, and he was happy.

I stopped suddenly. 'I don't want to go to the Taj,' I said. He looked at me with immediate understanding, something like approval. 'We'll see what we can find near the sea,' he said.

The taxi drove to the sea-front and we decided on a small hotel, more a guest house, with windows opening onto the sea. I don't remember who received us. Once in the room he put his arms around me, holding me to him. The familiar feel of his khaki jacket, the male smell of his hot body, the gentle stroking of my hair. He led me to the window where a breeze from the sea cooled the intense heat. We talked excitedly – about ourselves, our letters – enlarging what we had written, explaining, questioning.

In the afternoon we wandered about the shops of Bombay, indifferent to the sights and sounds around us, for as he wrote later 'enchantment sealed my forehead.' In the evening we went to the Juhu gardens 'to see the evening come to the little people'. Walking under the palm trees beside the beds of cannah lilies and salvia we felt at one with the strolling Indians, the women in their coloured saris, the men in their spotless white dhotis: they too had come to feel the cool breeze from off the sea. Still I did not tell him of the baby. I was not anxious – the time was not yet; it would come. As we strolled back to the hotel the moon came up over the sea and the waves fell onto the sand beneath the sea wall.

That night as Alun gently, tentatively, began to make love to me I felt a great tenderness for him, an anxious need to make true the reassurance I had innocently given him in the woods at Coonoor. Slowly I felt some uncertainty in him, some apprehension, lessen. The shy lover became confident, joyful. At the moment of his triumphant fulfilment he cried: 'I feel like a prince. Do I look like a prince?'

Later, as he lay quiet beside me, I told him of the baby. For a moment he did not move, then he got swiftly out of bed and went over to the window. He stood staring out at the sea. He wrote of this moment: 'I always thought then . . . of Philip Bossiney in *The Forsyte Saga*, when he was out in the fog and Soames was lord of the earth. It is a very wrong bad wicked feeling for me, & harmful . . . I couldn't help it Frieda. I had to feel it in the leaping wild panther part of me . . . It was . . . a kind of forest fire on my body, on my skin a bad burn.' After a time he turned and came back to where I sat on the edge of the bed. He put his arms around me. 'I'm glad,' he said and tears rushed to my eyes. 'I'm glad. I shall love him. Gilly's little brother.'

He did indeed love the unborn child. He became obsessed with the thought of it. He loved children and longed to be a father. He had a deeply sympathetic understanding of them. When he left the school in Wales where he had taught, his pupils presented him with a book in which they had inscribed: 'He understood us.' Gilly had inspired an especial love in him. My unborn baby became a source of mysterious emotion in him. He was convinced it was a boy. He was too gentle to state crudely that he wished it was his, but he longed for it to be and came near to convincing himself that it was in some mystic way. The child, a girl, was born two months after Alun's death. We named her Juliet. Many years after he died I learned that Alun had secretly, and known only to himself, given my unborn baby the name of Curig. I enquired about this unusual name and learned that Curig had been a Welsh-Saxon boy saint, martyred for his mother whose name, most curiously, was Juliet – a name unknown in Wales at that time.

In the days that followed he was touchingly careful of me. I was not very morning-sick, only possessed of a craving for bananas, which amused us both. We bought small green plantains – the Indian bananas – and we both ate them. Enchanted days when a chokra woke us with his bunch of lotus flowers and Alun would give him a few annas and put his hand upon his head – as he had upon Gilly's that first morning in Coonoor.

One evening we went to the Taj to dine and dance. An Indian servant, turbaned and wearing a red cummerbund around his long tunic, led us around the dance-floor to a table. Uniformed army officers and their wives or girlfriends sat at other tables in the subdued light, with here and there a plain-clothed businessman, alone or with a Eurasian woman from the more sophisticated levels of prostitution.

Alun ordered iced gimlets. With the cold stems of the glasses between our fingers we gazed across the table at each other. His deep-set dreaming eyes, the beautiful architrave of his brow, the black hair and the tentative lips which looked always as if they were about to speak or to smile and above which was a tiny scar. What did he see? Brown eyes, fair tawny hair, curving lips. The magic of love: the huge stillness.

We danced. The feel of khaki drill: the male smell of this particular man: my flowered summer dress, the springy feel of my hair, the scent of *Je Reviens* – sweet evocations of the great force which sweeps all else aside. The band stopped playing and we parted reluctantly to sit again at our table. There was a silly cabaret. We smiled at each other.

These are the happy memories when we were part of each other. There are also the sad memories, moments when he lived in his own shadowed world. One afternoon he read to me an article on Richard Hillary, the pilot burned horribly in an air battle and who was suspected of inviting his own ultimate death. The article was by Arthur Koestler who himself committed suicide in later life:

> The fraternity of the dead has its peculiar etiquette: one has not only to live up to one's form, one has to die up to it. But then again, there is the writer's curiosity which forces him to feel his own pulse, to jot down . . . the minutes of his agony;

there are the nerve-tearing oscillations between cant and introspection, acceptance and revolt, arrogance and humility, twenty-three years [Hillary's age] and eternity . . . When all isms become meaningless and the world an alley of crooked query marks, then indeed a man's longing for the Holy Grail may become so strong that he flies like a moth into the flame, and having burnt his wings, crawls back into it again.

Alun's voice broke as he read this to me. Reading it again fifty years later I am amazed that I did not at the time realise how exactly it described Alun's own preoccupation with death. I knew from his letters that he frequently thought of death, but his early letters were so joyful, so committed to life, that it was only after our meeting in Bombay that I realised the compelling nature of his obsession. He once wrote: 'I was naked splashing water over myself & singing this enormous and dreadful joy that came up to me so casually & said something quite final & terrible to me & I laughed and sang it back . . . I'm delighted that I can sing it & not shudder over it. I'll tell you about this, perhaps, if it's still in me in September in Bombay.'

I had not for a moment thought this 'final and terrible' joy was the acceptance of death. I thought it was some decision he had made about himself and me. If I had known what he had written in his journal at this time I would have understood: 'and last night I was singing under the shower . . . and there was my death quite clear and familiar at last after all the groping and revulsion and I sang of it in my tuneless man's voice.'

He then adds in his journal a curious, defiant passage: 'I will not add to those lecheries in the days that remain, nor hope less or love less, but more yea more and more love & ever love, & be less & less the nothing that does not exist & cannot breathe. I am glad & I am in love and I don't care.' (Quoted in John Pikoulis, *Alun Lewis: A Life*, Poetry Wales Press, 1984.)

On the morning of our departure the chokra brought his bunch of lotus flowers to our door as usual and Alun gave him a few extra annas and told him in pidgin English that we were leaving. The little fellow looked up at Alun with round sad eyes, glanced at our suitcases and then with a strange swift motion like the dipping of a bird's wing ran away.

We were silent in the taxi, Alun withdrawn, myself trying to hold fast the floodgates of tears at the sadness the chokra had so poignantly shown. I don't remember the train journey from Bombay to Poona, only and for ever the sight of Alun – the last time I would see him. He was not looking towards where I leaned out of the train window but stood with hunched shoulders, his head down as though awaiting the executioner's axe. Fear replaced sadness in me, at the realisation that his despair was not only at our parting but caused also by some darker emotion. If we had met in Bombay after I had received his later unhappy letters and not so soon after the first excited and joyful ones, my fear at this curious parting might have had some substance. As it was I was afraid that I was breaking up his life and all that had had meaning for him. I felt too that this despair would jeopardise our love.

How different the journey back to Mettapalyam was from the enchanted adventure I had set out upon five days earlier! I was tired and bereft: the beauty of the passing Indian landscape somehow emphasised my sense of loss: and a faint but pervasive guilt towards Alun because of the joy which I felt in the coming baby (and which despite my anxiety I could not suppress) – all this made the long hot dusty journey intolerable.

I had sent a telegram from Bombay asking that the car should meet me at Mettapalyam. As I was driven up the steep ghat road, the cool from the surrounding jungle a blessing after the baking heat of the plains, I felt empty of emotion, only aware of my tired body. Wallace had not yet returned from Delhi and Gilly was playing in the garden. As I embraced her, looking into her sweet face, a great wave of love swept over me for her, for the baby, for Wallace, for Alun; love in its gentleness, its compassion, its reassurance suddenly supplanted all else. Loss, anxiety, guilt, bewilderment were swept away by this sudden, all-enveloping love. It seemed so simple: love could not be measured – there was no longer a question of whom or how much one loved, love in itself was enough. It has many faces, I thought, each beautiful, and to accept love unquestioningly was to accept life in all its aspects. Alun later wrote something similar only, alas, his thoughts brought him no tranquil acceptance as they did me, only a further understanding of his despair.

Wallace returned and I told him I had gone to Poona to visit Dick but did not tell him of Bombay. He seemed surprised that I had left Coonoor – I so seldom did. The moment for which I had longed for so many years came when I told him I was pregnant. He looked steadily at me for a long moment then: 'I am so very glad,' he said and I knew he was as glad for himself as for me, for he had shared my long frustration and unhappiness.

The serenity I felt on my return faded as I began to live in two worlds, though its afterglow stayed with me until the end. I was preoccupied with preparation for my coming child, sewing, slowly putting together a layette, making a nursery – all this shared with Gilly and Wallace – and the joy of it. But I was still living partly in the world of love and closeness which belonged to Alun and me.

Alun's letters at this time did not comfort but worried me. His longing and need, his agonised awareness of loss would distress me but, more, his despair seemed shadowed by something other than these: a mysterious anxiety which seemed to be drawing him towards some void. I felt as helpless as he seemed to be. I wrote to him reassuring him of my love. His brave attempts to escape from the dark moods and to reassure himself that they were passing were heart-breaking. If I could have been with him to comfort him – but deep in me I knew that this darkness was something I could not share with him. I knew it to be more – much more – than the moodiness which occasionally assailed him.

He was a man of many moods. He knew this only too well. 'Oh God,' he wrote in an early letter, 'it [his love] will have all my many moods and failings in it.' And: 'you say often I am as rich as Croesus [in being a poet] & endowed with divine bounties at birth & it's only half true for I'm as poor as bloody old Lazarus and it's in poverty that you must find me if you love me.' In another letter he wrote: 'Frieda dearest, what have I said in my letters? Have I been tedious and muddling? I hurt sometimes in letters . . . it seems so spendthrift, writing things that pain when it's love that's inarticulate in you all the time your pen is writing . . . Don't let anything hurt you, Frieda, that I say. I'm not part of your hurt world. You know that, you told me so the night your eyes were wounded.'

He hurt me only once when I, puzzled, could not understand his own hurt in a letter which he had written while in hospital ill with malaria and what he called 'traffic jam' – bronchitis. I think it was written less from a dark mood than from illness. 'After twelve days of nothing I received your letter.' (Posts in India were very uncertain.) 'I'm sorry my long letter had to be how it was & you had to dig so deep and hard in replying to it.' What had I written to him? After fifty years I still read this letter with sadness. Had I told him not to be so despairing, so desperate? To be patient. 'I covet your patience,' he wrote. 'I only know that I'm sick of it' (his divided love for me and Gweno) 'hammering, hammering in my head.' I seem to have convinced him that I was impatient of his love, both in his letter and his poems. This, of course, was absurdly untrue, the very opposite of the truth: I was hungry for his assurance of love. It was his great love for me which evoked an answering love in myself. 'I'm sorry, because perhaps I've pestered you: and been fussy & foolishly impatient and too eager to find words and give hospitality to intuitions . . . And these poems' (he sent them to me for safe-keeping) 'are perpetuating them to your discomfort perhaps.' What could I have written? If only I had asked him to send my letters back to me when he asked what he should do with them at the end, when he was going into Burma, then I would know. This was the only letter I ever received from him which was not tender and loving. He tried to write again the next day, he told me, but was too ill to do so.

No doubt these occasional moods were connected with his depressive illness. Sometimes what seemed a change of mood sprang from his searing honesty. He was tough as well as honest – with himself and with others, even me, 'but not in our alley, Sally' – this when he thought I was enjoying some social occasion the implications of which he disapproved. 'You lunch with such Bulgarian monstrosities, Frieda, don't you?' These remarks touched me for I knew they were motivated by what Ian Hamilton in his study of Alun Lewis calls 'the uneasy side of him'. Uneasy maybe, but his unease was an expression of his compassion for the less privileged and his passionate commitment to Socialism. There was a bravery in his toughness. Writing of the coming confrontation with the Japanese he said: 'I'm no weakling and if endurance or one's own resources are all I need to get through any particular spot of murder I'm confident I can do it.' On more than one occasion he stood up to his superior officer – 'cooking my military goose' – and argued about what he saw as the truth. Once in the course of a lecture he was giving he refused to retract what an officer, who had entered the lecture room unexpectedly, demanded. The officer dismissed the class.

When he came out of hospital he wrote to me as he always had, but seemed increasingly unable to escape from the growing depression. He recognised its symptoms: 'my ancient enemy . . . Damn his bleary eyes.' In an earlier remarkable letter he described with imaginative detail the horror of the illness; it was a letter which haunted me and from which I first realised he was its victim. After he came out of hospital he wrote of it again. He said he had been unable to write before because 'It was simply the lack of toughness of my mind which I'm afraid isn't half as strong as I'd hoped and has really behaved very badly of late. It has been without conversation and without solace: a kind of deliberate impoverishment of all living streams, a shrinking and a despairing. I don't know why. But I've never been so cast off, so worthless, purposeless, unresponsive. I loathed myself for it and was anxious about it, too. I think it's shredding away a bit now, as the morning mist is shredding as I write from the deep lake below me in the hills.' The braveness in this letter and submission to the enemy he was powerless to resist filled me with a longing to take him in my arms and comfort him.

The anguish of the depressive is much to do with the fact that he hates himself: 'being such dross,' he wrote, 'I can't talk of belonging for worthlessness belongs to no one.' 'The culpa mea in it all.' 'Somehow I cast shadows wherever I go.' All this he wrote when depressed. And a most moving description of what life seemed to him and his attempt to live it as he felt it should be lived: 'Life is itself. I only guess at it and wonder & wonder & wonder. At its power, its waste & malevolence, its beauty and its flooding gifts. And if I fail, it is still itself. And if I try and try, and my failures are forgiven me, perhaps I will still make something of it.' These words are particularly poignant when one knows they were written by a man who gave himself wholly, without thought for his own health or relaxation, to his work in the army, to his creative talent and to the cherishing of the bonds of love for Gweno, his family, friends and me.

Despite the time and energy he gave to the troops, the intense 'self-stopping' army work – 'so many jobs, so many immediacies of Army & mucking in all the time' – and the pitiless and exhausting exercises and manoeuvres which took the battalion out to sea, over rivers, through jungle and for miles over the baking plains, he yet was able to write long wide-ranging letters to his friends, his family and to me. He wrote through the night. Nothing was ever superficial or lightly considered. He gave himself to the writing of his letters as unstintingly as he gave himself to all he did. Amazingly, after writing all night, he would turn to some idea forming in his mind, a draft poem perhaps or a story. 'It's midnight and I want to have a stab at the story I was thinking about during the week three midnights running.' Exhausted as he must have been, he was able to divert his creative energy from the long midnight letters to the composing of a poem or one of his remarkable short stories.

His depressions were infrequent and most of his life was lived in long periods of normality. But the remorseless way in which he drove himself at this time must have had much to do with his ill health and final depression. He seemed not to take seriously the doctors' conclusions that he had malaria or bronchitis, and he regarded dysentery as an inescapable part of tropical life. He endured the pain of his broken jaw and the operation but never talked about it – except to write a most significant poem about the hallucinations induced by the anaesthetic. He would do his utmost to get out of hospital while still unwell. He ate fitfully, often only because Harry Tudor, his faithful batman, brought him something to eat. I sent him vitamin pills (little used in those days) hoping he would take them.

I try to believe that all this combined with the sleepless nights and the exhausting military work and exercises are what destroyed him, and that his tormented love was only a part of it. But reluctantly I admit that it may have been the cause of his final depression. The possibility is anguish to me and I have prayed that it is only half true, knowing what all who knew him accept: that he would in due course have brought himself by his own hand to that world he wondered and dreamed about, which called him irresistibly. I find comfort in knowing that the delight and fulfilment he found in our love would cause him to choose to live that year over again, despite the anguish. There is also comfort in knowing that if he hadn't died he would have suffered greatly, because the battalion was decimated by the Japanese. If, as Intelligence Officer, he had been taken prisoner, he would have undergone torture.

He wrote to me: 'Frieda, I am full of peace because of you. You will remember that, please, won't you?' I have indeed remembered that.

Although his letters after we met in Bombay show his growing depression, there are those in which he seemed to emerge and enjoy what he was doing. (*The Times* obituarist wrote: 'His outlook was tragic but it was often penetrated by moments of radiance.' This was in reference to his poetry but it was also true of his realisation of life.) But I was dismayed by his last two letters for they were clearly written when the decision to take his own life had been made. In both he alternates between acceptance of the fact that he is going to die and slipping back into fleeting thoughts of a possible future. They are a testament of his agony. He was in the deepest depression, helpless yet determined to leave those he loved certain of his enduring love.

Before the battalion moved up into Burma he wrote letters to his parents, to Dick Mills and to me. They are not specifically farewell letters but the expectancy of death is in each of them. The one to his parents is full of loving determination to assure them of his love and gratitude for all they had done to make him what he was. It is calculated to read as a letter written before going into the dangers of battle. Those to Dick Mills and me show more clearly his pre-occupation with death. There is anxious excitement in his attempt to make clear his last thoughts, yet through the agitation runs a marsh light of an impossible hope that life might after all go on. 'I could have children with Frieda. Perhaps I will have children with

Gweno – I want them.' This fragmentation of his resolve must have been torture to him as he was relentlessly drawn towards his death.

On 11 February 1944 the South Wales Borderers joined a troop train going from Bombay to Calcutta. The entire battalion crowded into the train at Poona, from where it went on to Calcutta and from there to Chittagong, a journey in filthy carriages, when cooks would prepare food consisting of porridge and soya beside the line: a journey lasting for days, fly-tormented, in blinding heat, with dust which got into their hair, ears, eyes and into their mouths while they were eating.

Alun as an officer would have kept a brave face in these miserable circumstances, and no one would have guessed that he was in a state of agitation as he knew that death was now very rapidly approaching. The threat of death itself would not have obsessed him: all soldiers face the possibility of death. The cause of his inner frenzy lay in knowing the action he was to take in obedience to the relentless force which guided his will.

In physical and emotional chaos, and with the terrifying and certain prospect of confrontation with the Japanese, Alun yet found time to write to Gweno to reassure her and tell her, heart-breakingly, that his 'reason was taking control and working carefully and methodically'; that 'my grasp is broader and steadier than it's been for a long time'; and that their future must be 'full of sunlight and growth and health.' In fact, far from his reason taking control, he was on the perilous edge of breakdown. His journal shows that he was drawing nearer to suicide, counting the remaining days as 'twelve days that remain in a neat pile on a white cloth.'

To me he wrote in an agonised attempt to prove that so 'worthless' a creature as himself could 'belong' to no one. He wrote of 'returning to the revelation and incarnation', and that 'There is no end to all this, except the accidental end'. He then clearly describes his death. 'Oh the *thrill* of myself to thyself, sweet swordsman,' he wrote, 'the dancer & the dance, the wind & the cry of the wind.' His last words remain with me always: 'And I'll surely come up through the trees to the lawn to the splendour & the home-coming & the child & Gilly & us.'

I was driving Gilly home from a morning with a friend when we stopped the postman on his way to Highfield. He gave me several letters, amongst them one addressed in large simple handwriting. Puzzled, I glanced at it on the seat beside me several times. 'Who can it be from?' Gilly remembers me saying.

Wallace had come home for lunch and emerged from washing his hands in his bathroom to where I stood with the open letter in my hands. I was in the seventh month of my pregnancy and the christening robe, in which Wallace and then his brother had been christened, lay on the bed newly washed and ironed by Ayah and ready to be put in the layette basket. I read the letter, then turned sobbing into Wallace's arms. He took the letter from my hand and read it. He turned away, went out on to the verandah and leaned on the balcony rail.

'What a waste,' I heard him say. 'What a damned waste.'

My child was born, a girl. Alun in a letter had blessed '"his" little head.' She has all the graces such a blessing bestowed.

On my return to England I sat in Green Park with the baby in her pram beside me. I thought of Alun:

> Speak in me –
> Oh speak within my listening heart.
> I have waited on your teaching,
> Served so long your gentleness of thought.
> Silent, with love green-growing in my mind,
> I hear your voice, but far – so infinitely far.
> Today the Spring has moved the earth at last
> And alone and longing I cry out
> Oh speak in me.

Here are my "Twelve lines"

Where aloneness fiercely
Trumpets the unsounded night
And the silence surges higher
Than hands' or songs or mountain's height,

I the deep shaft sinking
Destroy the obdurate alone,
While with a willing anguish
You grow about me, flesh and bone.

The wild beast in the cave
Is all our pride: and cannot be
Again until the world's blind travail
Breaks in crimson flower from the tree
I am, in thee.

Frieda, it's so hard to think of you
packing you + gilly's clothes, laying your
diaphonous dust cover over, taking the
train to the sands, the warm sea,
I know I would be joyous if I came.
looking at your photographs of me I
was amazed at the absence of preoccupation
in me. I would break out of all this
to you. Instead I am going to sleep
myself into tomorrow.
        Goodnight darling. I hope you
are well.
        My love, Alun.

ALUN LEWIS LETTERS

All the letters to Freda Aykroyd were sent from ABPO 21 unless otherwise indicated

Dear Frieda,

Please excuse the Mrs. Ackroyd: Dick's made your Christian name the more natural one to use. I'm glad you're back home again: I cannot endure the thought of other people being in hospitals, though I found it a considerable experience myself.

Dick's just sent me a letter saying he's to come on leave on July 1st and that you have invited me as well. How could I spend my birthday better? But things aren't panning out that way and though it's 12 months since I had leave last, I can't get any till mid-August at the earliest. We've been working like a pack of welders in the Kayser ship yards for the last few months & are told there will be no let-up. So there we are. I'm very sorry for I would like to meet you very much. This Men only world gets tedious, and in India it seems that unless you have a nice staff job in a peaceful cantonment, the only female company you get you have to buy.

I feel very much at home in India for all that. My two brothers are both out here, one arriving last week; and I have an aunt who was the gingerbread house of my childhood, she's up in Darjeeling. Both my brothers are over that way, & I think I must go and call on them severally when I get my ten days off. I still don't despair of seeing you: maybe I'll come and convalesce there one day.

I had a day in Bombay yesterday which I enjoyed most sensuously. A hot bath, a swim, spending money on pugeree silk for wife, mother, and sister, buying books for the battalion, making a recording at Bombay radio of some of my poems & persuading them to play the record back to me – it really was a day and a bit. Have you heard your own voice? It's a most complex sensation, the Ego, the

Superego and the Id all outraged & abashed and flattered at the same time. I was mainly concerned with two things – to see whether I'd succeeded in cutting out the natural indolence of my normal voice, & to see whether I'd interpreted the rather intricate rhythms & stresses & significances which make up a poem's integrity. On the whole I was quite pleased with myself! Anyway, if it amuses you, you'll find a write-up in the *Listener* (India) sometime in July, & 15 minutes of a Welsh drawl to follow. I gave one reading on June 6th, but had no time to warn any of you.

Dick says you read the *N.S.& N.* review of my book. In fairness, I must ask you to read Elizabeth Bowen's or Edwin Muir's variations on the same theme. The trouble with *N.S.* reviewers, except Pritchett, is that they force everything into their own likeness. The guilt-complex of the isolated leftist intellectual engrossed in the escapist task of propagating political symptoms – who suffers from all that? Me or the reviewer? Not me, mister, I only got dysentery.

Please tell Dick I've written him a long letter more than a fortnight ago; it's sure to catch up with him so I won't plunge again into the thousand and one nights of my great ride in a 'Jeep' from Bombay to never mind where and back again. It was a wonderful job, that was – girls with camels & jungle walas with eyes like grapes & 200 miles a day on the mileometer & nice red rivers to swish our uncertain way across. How I love dak bungalows appearing at dusk & nothing but sleep & tomorrow in today's absorbing image. Tant pis, I'm back in the battalion again.

My brother who has just arrived sent me a very disturbing letter – his first child died when he was on embarkation leave – & *he refuses to believe it.* Oh Jesus Christ.

Well, Frieda, I hope you're taking life quietly and really mending. Look after yourself & give Dick a good rest too. I think he deserves it.

Auf wiedersehn, & many thanks for your hospitality,

Alun

214565 Lt Alun Lewis
6th Bn, South Wales Borderers
c/o Adv. Base P.O. 21

The first day

Freda,

I can't start any other way; and there are some words I cannot say. It's morning on Arkonam station. When I woke it was dark & I felt my finger throbbing where I'd stuck it into the electric fan last night, and I knew I'd gone and you'd gone. And in that caved-in sensation was also the other knowledge that sometimes the night plagues and tries to obscure, that I – & again it's hard to say, – love you, love you, love you.

I had ginger ale and tea with a Scotsman and a nurse & a sweet little subaltern with a dachshund he'd bought in Ooty for 100 chips (and fed on milk from a bottle and kissed it good night when he went to sleep in his pink silk pyjamas). And then I had a shower bath & washed my hair, and bought a paper & had my shoes cleaned and blessed the shoe-black's curly dirty hair. Last night there was an absurd demonstration from a waiting train we passed slowly – all the Indians booed & booed & booed – & I started cursing back at them & mocking them & laughing at them because they were only ganders who can hiss. But this morning the day is lovely & a bell is ringing in the town & the day has come very softly and unobtrusively on us and I can see & feel & hear you and speak to you, but not here, nor these words: but instead in your own woods, where the moles lie in the sunny water and you smile and, for all the world you know of, yet you are shy and very young, and innocent in a way you cannot hide.

I'm not looking for words, nor are words coming to me. I am sighing all the time, short of breath, and singing to myself the song from Rinaldo – 'Let me Weep' – though, I have no wish to weep but only to sing & dream.

This will reach you tomorrow – I won't be able to write more than a note at camp: and I won't write really till I get to Karachi on the 9th. I'm thankful for these days on the train. I tried to read Roger Fry yesterday but my mind rejects all other things as it rejected all things with you except the music and the delight.

Freda, beloved, things were queerly reversed and in a way it was a pity for yesterday* which hurts in me more than the finger with the blue nail coming off. But it was bitter, perhaps, for now there is no pretence in any sort, but only a beginning from the beginning; from the very beginning, darling, and not from where I left off in life with certain achievements.

I must get breakfast before the Bombay Mail comes in, though I still have no appetite. I'm glad you made me not-hungry, and that honey has no carbohydrates, fats or proteins.

Goodbye, little bee. x x x x Alun

---

* The incident in the wood: see page 34.

I may not write
till I reach Karachi
on the 9th

214565 *Lieut Alun Lewis,*
6th Bn, South Wales Borderers,
G.H.Q. Intelligence Course,
Old Government House,
Karachi.

August 5th

My darling Frieda,

I have never known less than I know now, the world being over-turned, and I must resist the desire to write of the things I don't know yet. If I say I've hardened suddenly, and yet am conscious of deep and vague obstructions and violences, I'm not clarifying anything or explaining anything. When I know how you are living I'll be better able to write to you. But I'm glad this fierce image has begun so soon in me to defy & deny and cozen and persuade: it may be that it's my mind, working in the lowest coal seams, examining ruthlessly the basis of the tranquillity which you filled me with, examining its implications, assessing its enormous costs. I find myself throwing up all sorts of answers & charges, none of which go deep enough. That tranquillity was so deep, I can't fathom it, and that ecstasy so unearthly that I can't answer it with the ordinary answers. I know I am involved utterly & entirely in what is happening, and I know that more depends upon it than just life; yet I am somehow as impartial as a battleground, and I wait as best I can. Another part of me actively seeks you, plans to meet you, fixes a time & a place which I couldn't ask you when we were together nor can I ask you with my pen now. Because it's hard to breathe now, Frieda, and there is nothing that can save today, darling, you not being here.

But I must try another way of writing to you, a way more tolerable & less painful than this half fearful attempt to realise the unbearable greatnesses you've suggested within me. A dud phrase keeps popping in my mind like a dead wood fire – 'The World Well

Lost' – It's a mocking phrase, and you know how it mocks, Frieda, don't you? So let's try the other way, through things.

First will you tell me some facts I'm wanting? The name of the Beethoven Quartet. The name of the Schumann concerto. The Italian words of the Rinaldo song & the name of the singer. Will you copy for me Yeats's poem 'Solomon and the Witch' from the red *Week-End Book*? It's a poem that has always meant more to me than I can say. When I found it on the last morning I realised how much I needed it. And how closely it foretold the broken rhythm of the wood where I could not help myself. I shall find it easier to pass the time, till you come to make Time one with Chance at last, if I have that poem in your handwriting. I want these facts because all that happened was so dissociated from time and place and obligation that I cannot keep it to earth, & they might help.

The journey started again after I'd posted your letter at Arkonam – a young Canadian and the Scotsman from Arranmore who was in the carriage at Coonoor and who saw me kiss you. And now he's gone & there is nobody who saw us. And I'm in camp & none of my thousand friends know anything at all of it. The journey went on all day & I read Roger Fry right through, admitting the many wise things that happened in his life, and particularly his courage in forbidding failures to compromise the fragile newborn successes that the future always offered him. His lost wife outlived him. That is the most significant fact in his life – as Virginia Woolf subtly puts it in a footnote. Her final eulogy was tedious: the best parts were always when she cleared herself out of the way & his own power filled each word. He was very courageous. I remember reading Gibbon's autobiography when I was in my neurotic twenty-first year & couldn't see any purpose in myself at all. Gibbon had achieved nothing, absolutely nothing, all he'd done was study coins & Roman history – and I felt the awful horror of having achieved nothing, never so intensely as then. I'd just got my M.A. & refused the Civil Service job & hated research more than anything else & had no purpose at all. It was as a matter of fact, my mother who pulled me together, in the dining room one day just before lunch when I suddenly & at last found words for it all & said 'I'm no good, mother, no good at all'. And thinking of Roger Fry's courage in following the tenuous and dubious lead which was all he had (& so much against) I realised with a momentary feeling of joy that I *did* discover the clue, the almost invisible clue, and followed it more ruthlessly than I realised. Robert Graves told me – & he's the only one to say so – that I'm not a 'war writer', but a 'writer': and the sooner the war ends the better for my writing. And it's quite true, for I write always *against* the tug of the war & the horror & tedium of it: and all I'm trying to write is love. And you made peace. And I wrote those poems of peace because you abolished the war for me. And I know it's a slick slipshod cliché that reviewers love to use when they say 'X is the best writer the war has produced', etc, when X is not a general but a poet, not a killer but a lover. I will only allow it to be true to say 'The war has produced a conscientious and sturdy platoon commander out of civilian X'. Christ, don't I *loathe* the bloody war? I hate it with my guts, because it's just plain rottenness and it has no satisfaction at all, either to the living or the being killed. But my tapeworm, my writing bug, he's alright. He's alive & obdurate, no matter how many other ways I fail. And I've got his courage to discard all death forms that these times seek to impose. And when I thought, reading old Roger Fry, of the long novels & plays I've written and thrown away, the blind persistence & humility of hammering at my typewriter in my mother's house while she dusted and cooked, & the utter lack of disappointment when I realised that 300 pages of typescript were no good – then I do know that I was right in trying just that, that, that, that. Anyway, he had the sense to follow his nose. Which *is* courage, no matter what the Puritans & the plutocrats & the prim think of it all.

After Fry had been cremated, I had dinner and climbed on to the top bank and read Wallace's *Three Philosophers* till I had finished it. It's difficult to speak of a book whose author is a living person to you. I think his style is most lucid and happy, his handling of ideas very possessed and masterly, and his evaluation of human qualities and events as clear and sound as the purely scientific side. Yet I feel he could have gone further, deeper into the men; it would have been less lucid, but more true. They are too 'easy' as they stand now in my mind, too recognisable & complete, too different from each other & everyone else. It's a sort of two-dimensional picture – Lavoisier I'm sure was more than that, very much more. He was never flat on a flat background. But I'm only thinking of harder ways of writing the book – and probably of spoiling it. I think it's a remarkable and good book & I wonder why he hasn't written more, despite all his other, more important *real* work, alleviating real suffering.

Well then I slept & when I woke there were the first houses of Poona rattling past. I washed & dressed & packed so hurriedly that I forgot my soap and toothbrush! Then I waited an hour for a truck, found one ultimately, and drove out here to the mud & the tents & the familiar faces & the brown flooded lake at noon. I drank a gin with Jack Gush & wanted to get drunk and felt possessed of excitement. Then I answered lots of questions about Ooty & was chivvied by the Colonel who's coming down there too – 'Come on Alun, what did you do? Can't you give me any addresses? etc etc' Bah!

All the afternoon & evening I was busy with battalion jobs – I never talked about the battalion, did I? – and it wasn't till dusk that I slipped away to look at the lake & feel the force of the water & know the flatness of the two hills on the other bank & the cloudy solidity of the great rock mountain of Sinn Garh, and the confidence & freedom of being by the water alone for five minutes. Then back to my tent to wash & change & have supper & more chivvying & creme de menthe & excuse me, please, I must write some letters & pack my kit. And my tent again, the hurricane lamp & the great pile of correspondence to wade through and the letters I've still to write although it's midnight now. Lloyd's Bank want to know when I'll clear the overdraft, the Army paymaster has charged me twice & must be told, Auntie Connie wrote 4 pages of minute descriptions of how she prepared my room & lunch & all the fruits she bought & the trains she met, because she somehow had the idea that I was arriving on the 22nd, and she asked all the officers on the trains if they'd seen me, and how the dogs, Simon & Red Ike, were expecting me, too. I must write to Auntie Connie, if writing is any use in these things. And two long letters from Glyn, tedious letters both, & two long letters from Huw, the little dashing quicksilver bugger that he is; and from Mother & Daddy that I've read, and nine from Gweno. And a lot of dud press cuttings that I've squeezed into little balls & hidden in a corner for the sweeper. I unpacked my tin box & fibre trunk and got together the books I want to send you – Rilke, Spender, Lawrence, (D.H. – poems), Don Gesualdo, the two books I borrowed from you, and the little Flying Officer X book, which I told Wallace to read & which I found by coincidence at Arkonam bookstall, and am sending to him. And *Raiders' Dawn* for you, Frieda.

And I've packed & sent the parcel & I was wretched at still not knowing whether it was 'Frieda' or 'Freda' – & I know it must be the former but I put 'Freda' in the book, so will you put a little 'i' in for me, Frieda darling? To stop me feeling 'diflas' about it. (Diflas is welsh – so is 'hiraeth' – various qualities of sadness my nation knows about.)

And there are still all these things to be done & a lorry to be loaded with my kit at 7.30 a.m. tomorrow morning. Then Bombay where I must buy furniture for the reading room I've set up in a hut here for the men, & American magazines, and writing paper & ink & drawing materials & chessmen. And the Gujerat mail towards Karachi in the evening. And there I'll have peace again.

69

And will you meet me, Frieda, and love me, and be loved by me? Will you exalt and exult me, you can do it so easily, so wholly? So holily. There's a little song I never sang to you, being so tranquil with you, by Purcell, do you know it?

> I attempt from Love's sickness to fly
> In vain
> Since I am myself my own fever and pain

You MUST write to me soooooooooon.
My address till Sept 8th is on page 1.
You MUST write. It's impossible to breathe otherwise.
And perhaps you'll send me a photograph? And you WILL send me your poems, Darling, I need them, too. I'm only talking of the things I really NEED. Christ, I need you.

> My dearest love
> In die ewigkeit
> Alun

214565 Lt. Alun Lewis
(6th S.W.B.) G.H.Q. 'I' School
Old Government House,
Karachi.

TAJ MAHAL HOTEL BOMBAY
5.30pm [August]

My Frieda

I said I wouldn't write till I got to Karachi; this is therefore a lie! But I've finished spending the Army's money to the tune of Rs 150 on furniture & chess & books and I've got an hour before I need go to the station. So I came in to the Taj for tea and a bath and a little note to you.

How are you, Frieda? Are you well, beautiful, happy, gay, tired, doubtful, lost, depressed, elated – what? Oh, if I could *see* you; I've been wanting you all day, from before I woke. So much did I so that I suddenly told the driver of the three ton lorry we were going to Bombay in to get into my seat and I drove all the way in, over 100 miles, in four hours; playing ducks and drakes with convoys of new lorries going up from the docks & trails of learner lorries that wobbled in sheer hysteria when I ground past. I'm a fairly good driver, but I haven't had a lot of experience – the main thing is that I keep as cool as ice; and always have done when it's a question of quick judgment as opposed to nervous & imaginative thought. I got so immersed in judging speeds & cut-ins and passing that I held the most tranquil reverie with you all the way down.

It took me two hours to buy the furniture & stuff – now it's 5.30 p.m. I also bought a copy of *Last Inspection*, so you can keep the one I left with you, although I'd like to 'write' in it; but perhaps I'll come to Coonoor again. I'm worried as to whether I'll see you again, Frieda. If you were to come to Poona at the end of Dick's course, & then come on to Bombay on *Sept. 14th* & I contrived a few days' leave from Karachi – though I fear mid September will be a bad time as far as the regiment is concerned. Or if you could come to Poona in October or November – could you, darling? I shouldn't be asking you, I'm sorry.

Will you send me some poetry to Karachi? With your Beveridge work and the poems you're so shy about. Send me Hayward's Anthology of C18th poems, or *The Week-End Book*. I tried to buy a complete Yeats for you here but the shop in which I saw a copy has sold it. The book shops are good here but I haven't time to go round them all, & I've bought nothing for the train so maybe I'll read Army pamphlets instead.

I would like the Rilke sometime, because he's always fresh to read. I want to write some more poems, but I can't, not yet, because I'm only slowly perceiving how different everything is from anything that went before. I'm so tired of travelling away from you, and I didn't try to sleep last night till I'd read all my letters & replied to them, so no wonder I woke up feeling morose.

Yet I'm very, very happy somewhere – you may know where – do you?

Alun

In a Railway Train, 214565 *Lt A Lewis*
Delhi Junction. 6 *SWB*
'It was good enough *GHQ 'I' School*
for Foch.' *Old Government House*
 Karachi

Sunday night (8th) [August]

Frieda Darling,

Tonight I am discovered at Delhi Junction, still as far from Karachi as I was when I started the journey three days ago. I've become a regular train louse now and never want to arrive but simply go on feeling more & more sluggish and liverish and anonymous till I've become identical with the frozen furniture of the railway restaurants in which I daily appear. Except of course that soon I'll have no money left & will have to wash dishes to obtain a meal.

I think perpetually of you, darling, and through you I am enamoured of this no-world of the railway train where thought is free & has its own time. That's why I really don't want the journey to end.

I'm three days late for my course – so it's as well that the result won't materially affect me – for once in a while I don't want to do well, despite the natural instinct to do a thing well for its own sake. I want to be with my own gang when the bad dreams become a series of reverberant facts. So many of the men are from my own home, were taught by my father or delivered groceries to the house, or worked with my Orphean uncle in Shepherd's pit or Brown's pit. I do belong to them for this war and I always think of the peace in terms of their job, & their kids. I always feel glad when I'm part of them.

The train looks like starting; I've been living from hand to mouth on this trip. It all started wrong at Bombay. I put my luggage in Victoria Station and after buying furniture & writing to Frieda I called on two friends from the regiment who were on leave. It was a bit late then. We drank a few gins & ate peanuts & it got really late. Then I made for the station & met my old batman, Harry Tudor, a bald little merchant navy man with eyes of blue ice. He was the first to discover my train went from Central Station. I remember having sufficient gin in me to commandeer a taxi which had a nice comfortable ICS man and his baggage in it. And I just got onto the train in time. The next day there were floods & I had to switch onto a crawling monster of a train that finally landed me here at midday with a belly full of curry & rice and a mild tannic poisoning resulting from the attempts I made to extinguish the curry. I didn't feel like seeing Delhi, but persuaded myself to take a tonga to the places you're supposed to see – to wit Jama Mosque and the Fort. It was thoroughly unpleasant – the tonga walas & guides are so bloody rude & corrupt: the snivelling little magister who collared me at the gateway of the Fort and told me he'd taken Chiang Kai Shek & 500 schoolchildren round (and offered to give me 5 rupees worth of history or 50 rupees of the same & who said his heart was broken when I eventually coughed up two chips to get rid of the old dredger). And the horrible relics of Mahomet, the hair of his head & the sandal & the print of his foot on stone all bottled up in a black little reliquary with a written chitty from the C-I-C saying he saw the relics in 1914 & enjoyed them very much. Oouch! Je m'en fiche. I went & had a look at St. James within the Kashmir gate, too – a catholic church whose bells called me – I felt sad I wasn't a Catholic for I had great desire to be comforted. The lights are failing now (as Sir Edward Grey once muttered) and I'd better retire gracefully, after saying I had a bath & a meal in the evening and wrote a poem in the morning and loved you and loved you and loved you all the day. The lights are a bit better, and I'll write the poem on the last page. All today I've been thinking of the lake. What did it all mean? How did it do so much? The only answer is in your eyes and in your lips.

The Return

Six days and two thousand miles
I have watched the shafted rain
Feminise the burning land
Cloaking with a green distress
The cerulean and the ochre
Of the season's ruthlessness.

Six days and two thousand miles
I have gone alone
With a green mind and with you
Blazing in the stubborn bone.

Soldiers quickened by your breath
Feel the sudden spur and rush
Of the life they put away
Lest the war should break & crush
Beauties more profound than death.

And, swimming in the naked lake
I breasted with exquisite ease
The foaming arabesques of joy
And in the sarabande of trees
Of guava and papaya
And crimson blown poinsettia,
Like a lark within its nest
Laid my hand upon your breast,
[one line deleted by A.L.]
But the iron beasts deploy
And all my effort is my fate,
With gladiators and levies,
All laconic disciplined men,
I pass beyond your golden gate
To murder & destroy.

THE RETURN.

Six days and two thousand miles
I have watched the shafted rain
Feminise the burning land
Cloaking with a green distress
The cerulean and the ochre
Of the season's ruthlessness.

Six days & two thousand miles
I have gone alone
With a green mind and with you
Blazing in the stubborn bone.

Soldiers quickened by your breath
Feel the sudden spur and rush
Of the life they put away
Lest the war should break & crush
Beauties more profound than death.

And swimming in the naked lake
I breasted with exquisite ease
The foaming arabesques of joy
And in the sarabande of trees,
Of guava and papaya
And crimson blown poinsettia,
Like a lark within its nest
Laid my hand upon your breast,

But the iron beasts deploy
And all my effort is my fate,
With gladiators and levies,
All laconic disciplined men,
I pass beyond your golden gate
To murder & destroy.
And in the ~~long~~ (darkness of the world)
And in the brilliance of this pain
I exult with such a passion
To be squandered, to be burned
To be joined with you again.

And in the [two words deleted by A.L.]
   hardness of the world
And in the brilliance of this pain
I exult with such a passion
To be squandered, to be hurled
To be joined with you again.

Please tell Gilly I miss
her a very great deal.
I do indeed, I love Gilly.
Life must delight in her, for
she gives so perfect a response.
In a way she is Life, the sifted
pure Life which
is the only Life that matters. Of course

214565 Lt. A Lewis
(6 S.W.B.)
GHQ Intelligence School
KARACHI

11th August 43.

Frieda Darling,

This is the first evening, and the longest day since the first day I went to boarding school back in 1926. I don't know precisely why I have this loathing. Creature comforts abound – I'm writing in a basket chair on a pseudo-marble terrace above a lawn, having had a hot bath and a gin & awaiting dinner – and I hate it like hell, just like hell! All of it. I had to cycle into Karachi (this place is on the fringe) to get an identification photograph & met some young Americans – they said 'Do you like Karachi, brother?' 'I haven't see it yet', says I 'and I hate it like poison'.

Enough of that, it doesn't count anyway. I've a shrewd idea what is really happening, and how organically it's connected with the utter release of your trees and skies and presence, so it would be a bit unkind to Karachi to describe it with this jaundiced eye. I was given your telegram in the middle of the wilderness this morning and I've clung to it all day. Thank you for sending it to me. I needed it like hell. I don't know why my letter took so long. I posted it on the 6th and it should have flown if the wish & the will have any power in the world of affairs. I wrote to you also from Arkonam, and on Sunday from Delhi. I think of you all the bloody time. Do you mind?

That was dinner. And this is the Secret Information Room. It's a hive of pamphlets and maps and a few rather nice books such as *Western Influences on Japanese Culture* etc. They've given us a mort of work, if one were to do it all. I find people as feverish as students in the swot-fortnight before sessionals, but I'm not getting het up myself. The amount of literature & homework problems they throw at us is curiously at variance with the faces of the instructors – there's one Inniskilling Major here, maybe you know him, Major Wilson? Il fait des sottises formidables: I don't know where the new & the vigorous concept is: I imagine it in terms of Robert Graves's poem on Laura Riding – if there were omens at her birth he would not wonder

> 'Being tourbillions in time made
> By the pulling of her bladed mind.'

Do you like my Rilke? Have you read 'Nike'?

> 'And did the hero feel her weight?'

He's grown in & through me and I've had to exorcise him, for he becomes a bad influence in the writing of poetry – he cuts away your strength after a time, and the translator had a vapid undertone that emerges if you read him too often. But it's a wonderful book. I'm sure you'll like Spender – he has the same effect as a cold shower after a bad night – like strolling into a Van Gogh after spending a few hours among the Renaissance artists in the National Gallery. What else did I send you? *Raiders' Dawn* – poor little *Raiders' Dawn*. It's not a *bad* book is it, but it's a very young one. Full of seed, every page is seed; no harvest, only seed, seed, seed.

I do want you to criticise what I write, Frieda, I never need praise except when it's a new thing that I've just written & is still part of my flesh & blood – like 'The Orange Grove', – it will detach itself in time & I'll want it to be criticised & I'll want to perfect it – but now it's still part of me & I can no more perfect it than I can perfect myself. I've written out the poems I read to you in embryo – 'The Journey' & 'The Gateway of India'; and rewritten the little peasant poem 'The Field'*; and written another full of hurt which I don't know whether to send you or not. But I wasn't able to write in the train – I was too much flux. When I think of it, I think the poems are an act of daring, always daring, to plunge & tear & enter; & the stories are an act of recognition & steadiness, of *myself where I am*. Is that true? I value the stories myself because they stick to things the poetry sweeps above or below. They authenticate the poems; pay for them in cash or sweat or patience or guts or belief or disbelief: That's why I asked you to read the stories as *me*. I don't often do that, or realise it. And when people read my book I'm quite indifferent & never feel there is any incursion on my privacy. But if you read them I want them to be me for you – & I know you'll understand. They aren't me clinically – I'm not Flick or The Children or the boy in 'It's a Long Way to Go', nor is Gweno Gracie. I'm not even me in 'Lance-Jack', in the sex-hunger wretchednesses – for when I wrote it I was living in the most divinely satisfying sin, but there was always the other world, the hungry pale planet of loneliness,

*See below, page 91.

the natural failures. I don't want to make too much of them, Frieda; I never do, except when suddenly someone makes my whole life swing into one single orbit and I am compelled to integrate these worlds more closely because I feel all their strength swinging me the way of that person. And that doesn't happen often. How many times in a life time?

There are many things I can't talk about now, but you will understand that, won't you? God, this uncanny understanding – so close that it becomes invisible, immanent, unnecessary. When I saw you on Saturday July 24th you were the flash of a sword and I was bewildered and very tranquil. I got my kit out of the taxi & paid the taxi & strolled back to the verandah & waited for you. I don't think I have ever been as innocent as I was then. Innocence is a hell of a damned thing to suffer from; it's much easier to be a doggy man & slink about with a nice natural greed & the intention of satisfying it. I see very clearly the slavering face of that drunk major in a kilt making passes at Gloria in the Club; sex just dripping off his face like lard or shaving lather. If he'd come slavering round you I think I'd have hit him.

Good night, Frieda darling. My love & thoughts, Alun.

This course goes on to
the 19th *of Sept, Frieda,*
so the trinity still can't
meet. Not just yet, anyway.
Will you lend me Texts &
Pretexts (*Huxley*) *and*
Zola's Germinal?

214565 Lieut. A. Lewis
(6 S.W.B.)
GHQ Intelligence School
KARACHI

Sunday 15 Aug

Frieda darling,

I've just looked in my locker for your letter, and it still isn't there. Yesterday there was one from Dick. I want yours so much that I'll find it difficult to open it, when I do at last hold it. Yet even at this drowsy mid day with cawing rooks & the sound of cars on the highway I can feel you thinking and can work with you through the enormous canyons by the difficult way that's been our luck.

> How shall I your true love know
> From another one?
> By his cockle hat and staff
> And his silver shoon.

Dick's letter was either amazingly brave or amazingly ingenuous. In either case amazing. I am somehow tied up in the way of things and cannot share his clear and vigorous belief in ourselves – you have produced a clarification in Dick, and an impetus, and the warmth that is necessary for belief – and it's possible only when a relationship is clear and moving & warm. Dick loves you that way. I love you some other way, oh many other ways, I don't know how many, but just now I love you with a constriction of the heart, as if you were holding it, tight, tight, and everything that will emerge from that microcosm is enclosed in spun silk inside it. It's in the constriction that the hurt lies; there are more obvious fields of hurt moving against each other, too, a sort of dualism that goes right through, and I've been trying very hard to find out what has happened in me now. I was afraid there'd been a huge destruction but perhaps there hasn't been, after all. We hanker after one-ness, it's the dominant urge – monotheism, monogamy, the uniquely beloved whose face and body is always immanent in distance and danger & despondency and the homeward dream – and I only slowly admit to myself that my whole being has other loyalties or at least other ways of attaining the consummation that Rilke calls a harmony between the individual & the universal cycle of beauty. Whenever I see a lake or a river or a bay whose beauty pierces me I merge with it, become it. In the activity of living I know now that I've always wanted and longed for another and another illumination, to encounter and know and merge with the same living stream in whoever it flows. In you, and you, and you. In childhood, boyhood, manhood, in time and out of time. Why should that hurt? Because somehow it is hurting others: it hurts the possessive in others, wounds them, distresses & confounds them. And all words, all explanations are hard & hurtful & I shrink from such words or the labour of making them audible and cogent. So when you said you wished to be alone I answered 'Yes yes yes' with my whole heart, but my voice said 'No' aloud. Because I was afraid of the thoughts that would come, and become a resolve ultimately, and after that become words spoken to someone else, someone very very important & easy also to hurt. Yet the deepest longing *is* this aloneness that we need, and I gladly go into it, very gladly, although I fear it also. I fear it for the simple reason that it isn't final, that one cannot stay there, but must emerge, and *must obey* what it insists. I've always refused to submit to a rule – Jesuit, Anglican, Nonconformist, military – out of fear: and I've clung as long as possible to the freedom that does not decide and scarcely has an opinion, that suddenly acts from an overpowering conviction that appears to be simple intuition, and acts always *in* the situation, and not according to rules that one applies to the situation. Yesterday I was cycling along a desert track and I wished I was a Catholic, like I did hearing the bells & seeing the people & the priest in his soutane at doors of the Church of St. James within the Kashmir Gate at Old Delhi. But I never will. My true self spoke very well for me the morning I woke up as the train was running towards Lahore. I slept till 8.30 and in my sleep the occupants of the carriage left and when I awoke my eyes gazed at the only occupant then, an old emaciated Catholic priest in a grey drill soutane with silver rimmed spectacles and a long thin white beard. I lay & gazed at him for ten minutes, then I said 'Good morning, father', and he smiled back. I washed & shaved & dressed and came back to speak to him. I asked him whether he liked the dry villages better than his native Belgium, and he said No. He said India wearied him and he was glad to be going to Lahore to discuss the world with his priestly superior, and it was like a holiday to him. Then he asked me a lot of questions and I said I had no religion but I had a belief in humanity. And he said 'Perhaps it is harder for you. You do not have my consolations.' I said 'No I haven't *your* consolations, father, but I'm as utterly in the hands of life as you are and as free to be driven or guided as it may be.' Then we talked of the war & communism and he gave me some little pamphlets and patted my leg as if I were a little puppy when he left the train. And I felt incredibly happy after talking to the little father. Is it that I confessed myself to him? Without realising it? Or that I merely wanted him to understand how the soldier can be as selfless as the priest?

My trouble is that I think big and try big always. I've always lacked patience for the small things, looking for a key I've misplaced or writing an easy story or making it an easy war or letting love be easy. And if I fail, as I constantly do, it may be humiliating, and it may make others laugh a bit jeeringly. It is also humiliating to fail through one's own deficiencies. But I don't see any other way of using my life and I'll try the biggest thing I can imagine myself doing, whatever it is. As far as the fighting goes, it's just being a good officer with the men, solid with the men. As for the peace, it's doing my bloody hardest in any way from street corner speaking to stumping or writing or fighting or persuading. As for writing, it's to write under inner vision only & never for money or name. As for love – but it's hard writing this, and anyway you know what I am and we ought to be laughing and glad of ourselves. Will we ever write a play together? I've written four that I've got stuffed away in envelopes at home, and they're like the stories I write & wrote & the two novels – just preparation. I will write a play one day – I'd love to write it with you, & act it as we think & work & argue & hammer, and go off on my own and come back again with another line written or a scene shifted. Will I see you acting? My bum would be very hot to sit on that night. [. . .].

I don't want to talk about Karachi or work or play. Time is full of it at the moment though I've scarcely noticed it. I had my first flight in an aeroplane on Friday evening. It was very queer – the world looks like Shangri La. There is a little tree-encircled leper colony between two hills in the desert. We circled over it & I had to identify it on my map. My heart went down to it. Yesterday I was dropped in the desert off a truck with sandwiches & water & a bicycle to look for landing grounds. The desert is a wonderful place, full of sterility & mirages. I came upon a native graveyard, and the camels with packs of brushwood were like avenues of poplars and I saw nothing living except cactus and lizards. I followed a camel track saying Salaam to the camel drivers, and came to the sea, the blue old sea churning away on the rocks all wet & beautiful, and three pi dogs yowling at me till I went.

Last night I went to the Gymkhana Club & watched people dancing & drank a villainous rum & was very tranquil and had a nice officer who was Assistant Military Attaché at Tokyo to talk to about Wales (he's Welsh & has forgotten it). This morning I cycled down to the Boat Club to swim in a relay race which we lost & there were more people to look at tranquilly again. I don't want to talk to them, just please look at them. This evening I must do more work. I have to 'speak' tomorrow – a) about Gandhi and b) about being a Battalion Intelligence Officer. They're playing Beethoven's 7th & Dvorak's Cello Concerto tonight on the gramophone.

Goodbye once again, my pen says, but not me.

Dear Frieda
My love
Alun

214565 *Lieut. A. Lewis*
(*6SWB*)
GHQ Intelligence School
KARACHI

17th *Tuesday*

Frieda beloved,

Oh such wealth, great caskets of sunlight unlocked pouring all over me like the water in the lake – *all* your letters – three envelopes of your letters – all waiting there today. Darling, darling, darling Frieda, making me feel so many multitudes in my heart & thoughts and manness and one deep mood after another gravely approaching and in a brave pattern dancing. This clearness you give me at the end, as Bach could, and Beethoven and Purcell. There isn't anything I can do with this fullness except feel it and bless it – do I need to *convey* it to you, darling? It is yours already, isn't it? Surely, more soon than it's become mine. But I, too, would throw you like a lasso, and laugh, laugh, laugh. I would also be utterly quiet, utterly devout. Do you know? There are situations, obligations, yes, yes, yes – but not now: nor when we meet again. Nothing then except what you have told me and I cry back to you in music and not words —— Frieda, come to me. It doesn't matter when. Perhaps you won't be able to till you've been to hospital – darling, I'm awfully pinched & sorry & bothered at your illness – & perhaps I won't be able to come till I've been to Burma. Don't think I'm philosophising the summum bonum of body and eye & embrace out through the hole in the top of the head when I say it doesn't matter when. I shall want you *every* day, sometimes with a hunger whose frustration is savage – but when it happens it will be happening for now and for ever. And Time couldn't much alter the truth, but only the when. Let him have his when. If only you say you'll come when we can.

Frieda dearest, what have I said in my letters? Have I been tedious or muddling? I hurt sometimes in letters, I hurt Marjorie once bitterly in a letter I had no control over: she wrote a stinging nettle back – it seems so spendthrift, writing things that pain when it's love that's inarticulate in you all the time your pen is writhing. I write what I must, none the less. Don't let anything hurt you, Frieda, that I say. I'm not part of your hurt world. You know that, you told me so the night your eyes were wounded. Oh bless all you say in your letters. May I just be disjointed a minute?

The darling colonel, could he respect you so much as to say that he was sad for you? I hope we see him again & again. Dick & you – damn you both for me not being there – I want to feel with you both, toss profundities into the air with you *both*. Damn you both. I *can't* meet him at Poona, sweet; I'm not leaving here till the 19th – Bombay the 21st. Damn you both, you buggers. There, that's like a young Indian officer with a perfect mastery of the English! Oh damn damn damn you both, I'm as happy & crazy and serious as God the Father God the Son and God the buttered toast. I love & I love & I love, so damn you both. Do you know? How I love? What ways? What pretty ways? sometimes? Sometimes I love very badly, Frieda Buttercups. Where am I? I'm by the green salty river in empty Karachi Boat Club, windy in the evening, the prevailing wind taking the guts out of the sun and rows of derricks above the transit sheds & wharves.

The day I went: the gramophone I left open & the records I left half played & I knew you'd see them when you came back. I don't mean I left them by design, as a pang! It's always like that when I go away, that's all. I just have to run like a wildcat to catch the train. I ran all the way across London last time I was at Howell's in Highgate – I left in the middle of the second movement of a later Beethoven quartet – & Howell who doesn't say personal things ever but fills his letter with the world & dreams, he said in the letter he wrote after I'd run away 'Your coffee cup isn't drunk & the third movement isn't completed? Isn't it legitimate to finish a cup of coffee & complete a quartet? Surely it's sad if life prevents such innocent things?' So I don't *think* about going till – poof! I'm gone you see. But when we move as a regiment, oh then we organise everything and clear up everything & go spotlessly, leaving absolutely no trace of our identity at all. We burn ourselves in the incinerator & bury ourselves in trenches and march out in good order. And then we are no longer there.

But I am still in you

I love your poems, Frieda, I do honestly. You can write poetry as well as being a poet – the writing is just something very difficult that one is able or unable to do – like breaking a cipher or a quadratic – but the being a poet is a lovely thing – God what *repose* I found in you, Frieda, that Saturday night when they all went and I knew your silky hair on my cheek at last, at first.

I don't want to do anything with your poems except read & feel them. Won't you send me more on those conditions? I'm not an old schoolmaster at all at all.

Why should, how could I hate you? You are a fool, Frieda, oh such a fool. How could I, you beautiful beautiful old goose? you child. May I please kiss you now?

The last letter I wrote on Sunday had a lot of fear in it, & pain. There's no fear or pain in this one. Is it any the less or more true for that? Gweno has a lot of fear – sometimes I have a bit, for the Japs, & the helplessness there is in it & and it's very salutary to fear a divebomber – but not too much. I'm not really afraid of anything except spoiling somebody else for what their good is. The other fears are not compulsive – they only guide and test me all the time. I'm not afraid of you – I did kiss you like a brother, as I too kissed Mair last time I saw her off on a train – and I will be very careful, Frieda, though there is no *need* to be careful. It won't break – Like I told you how to squeeze an egg, see?

Oh Christ I want more & more & more, much more. I'm terribly hungry and thirsty. I'm not writing anything now, neither poem nor story. If we were both here or both where you are I'd write – given time I'd write purely – I'd have a mind like stones in a clear pool, smooth & clean & rough-smooth & coloured – you could so purify my mind & rid me of all the noises and improvisations I'm forced to make shift with, because there are so many jobs, so many immediacies of Army & mucking-in all the time: if we could be free of those for – oh how long? I don't know how long. Then I would write. I don't know how I've continued to write the little I have. I've always had to push a pile of things out of the way to have room enough to write a little. I dream of this other time, of deep freedom ———

Something absolute about us makes it hard to write. Can I add to it or take away or do anything at all to it? I know I can't. I'm going to swim now, darling. And dive with a queer hesitation in my tummy. I'm very badly in love with you, just as a matter of fact & there's some dance music started inside. I bought 'It Still Suits Me' yesterday so you needn't be without it, & all I want is to kiss you & be with you all day & all night. Please don't be ill, darling.

My dearest love.

Back in the house:
Don't be ill, Frieda. I've had a long strong swim. It was slappy water, very salty, & big silver fish jumping, & I've cycled back to this characterless insipid empty house where I share the tiled floor with two other men & someone else has a gramophone upstairs. Shall I ask them to play 'It Still Suits Me'? It would be fun, wouldn't it? If you *are* ill, be tranquil, darling. Come & see me when you're strong again, if I can't come to see you when you're ill. It's awfully hard to get away from the Battalion – the week I had with you is the only leave we've been allowed & we're committed to the hilt in the future.

I do grieve. I know that. I don't let myself hate because hate spoils – it withers & shrinks like socks in salt water, but grief pours gentleness liquidly round everything and it's a natural expression for the love & the melancholy humour that almost, I think, I like best.

I'll copy out 'The Field' for you as I've altered it – and the other one 'Love'. Darling I could go on writing for ever, but here & now I must stop writing.

Don't worry about my love, will you, or your own love?

Hands are safe, are gentle, are kind.

Please write to me the most

Ever your

Alun

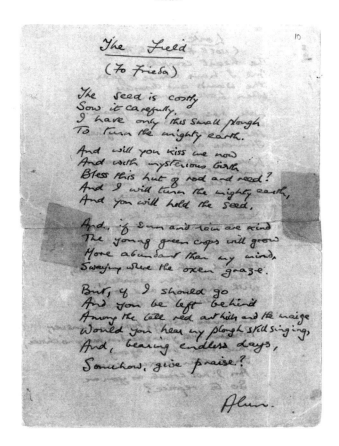

214565 Lieut A Lewis
(6ᵗʰ SWB)
GHQ Intelligence School
Old Govt. House
KARACHI

19ᵗʰ Thursday

Frieda darling,

Still wealthy, I've had three letters from you since I wrote to you the night before last – one yesterday and two today. Today's made me feel happy, but yesterday's distressed me as much as you said it might. And so, when I was sitting & writing to you on Sunday, you were going through all the horrible submission and retching sickness. Poor Frieda, I've tried to reach you, and be with you, I could comfort you so, just being with you – comfort you more than Dick or Jack Gush when I was real bad the first septic week, and they were so delightful just being there except that I was so tired of the morphia & sulphanilomide. I pray that you're reading this in your own tall house, and that the internal wound is healing quietly, and your mind or emotions or womanhood are not paining you also all the time. I didn't know, Frieda, nor does your letter make it clear: nor do I want you to explain anything of it to me. For some reason or other I shy away like a mettlesome horse from - - I'm not looking for names for it. I only know you're ill and it's something vital and I want you to be rid of it. Look after all of yourself, darling. You tell me to. O.K. I'm telling you. You're headstrong: maybe you'll pay as much attention to warnings as I do. I do hope you're better Frieda dear.

Today's little letters were nice ones, except the great bludgeon blow you struck about *my* death. Damn you, Frieda Buttery, don't say such a thing! You don't know. And you say it almost as if it would be my fault, for being clumsy, or not worldly wise enough.

There's a devil of a lot of very skilful and wise people gone clean out of existence since 1939, they're a company not to be ashamed of. And I'm not clumsy and I am moderately wise to the world. Wise enough to know that there are a lot of risks I can't avoid, and wise enough to know I don't want to avoid them. I *want* to run the gamut; and it's quite a mature wish, too: – it isn't for the thrill of it nor for the horror of it, though both these attract. It's for two reasons – to have authority in the long fight of peace, and to share the comradeship of a war, and of death. Sounds very British Legion, to write it: still, it's sound enough. As for death, it's a matter of luck. I'm no weakling and if endurance or one's own resources are all I need to get through any particular spot of murder I'm confident I can do it. But I *do* think of death a great deal, and I think life and human relationships have grown more & more precious & warm and urgent to me because of this thought at the back of everything. I'm not taking life on the cheap because its lease is doubtful – on the contrary I value every good & every joy & every loyalty I feel in it more highly than I could before; and I'm less nihilistic than I've ever been. All of which is a bit contradictory, but who isn't?

I'm glad you liked the poem, Frieda. I hadn't read it since I wrote it – I read it this afternoon and it seemed strange that it should be there, clear and hard as a lump of coal, and of that long euthanasia of the train that that should be there. I imagine a mother looks at her child in some moods and is incredulous that she has borne it. I like best to abstract my own self out of a poem & feel 'I didn't write it. It was only my hand that wrote it. It wrote itself, being a sponta-neous action in the world of thought'. And similarly to submit myself to a poem, offering it hospitality, and respect; if it wishes to be written by me I'll help it. Often I think of Love the same way. I don't love all the time – I'm not big enough; but I honour it all the time and wait for it, wait for myself to be of its own stature and rhythm. But not possessive about it, not claiming a right and feeling a hell of a great guy – not that I wasn't bloody proud of your hand on my arm in Coonoor or pirouetting you on the dance floor or splitting a pot of coffee with you in Davies's. Surely I was proud of you, of myself – but that's only the colour on the finch's crest. The other, deeper existence, is it not a purification & submission? Tell me I'm talking too much.

I'm in my cheap swimming trunks again this evening, at the Boat Club. I got very fed up with the eternal yapyapyap of the classroom and my mind didn't want to wrap itself round the dry techniques of war. This little circle of nothing is a relief from the sterile discussions of those professional bureaucrats-de-guerre. Though even here I'm infuriated with two Americans talking shop in loud voices next door to me. Frieda, would it be nice to take you to Kashmir? It sounds lovely, fine handicrafts and long inland waterways and flowers and the luxe, calme et volupté of a drifting houseboat – not this year, not next year, maybe. I'd like to go there with you, Frieda, more than anything else I can think of at all anywhere anytime. Except perhaps getting into a pile of realities in London and South Wales, which would also be very very good. But I would like Kashmir with you. There's a poem in that little Lawrence I sent you, written on a balcony over a Bavarian river. Read it for what I mean, will you? Maybe I'll get another leave, though, next year sometime. CAN you come to Kashmir with me? X X X X

Thank you for the two books, darling. I shouldn't have asked for the other two as well – pestering you for books. Don't bother to send them, Miss. But the poems in *The Week-End Book* are good – I read the 'Song of Solomon' last night – Cripes! How true it is, the simple physical truths it tells. 'My breasts are like towers.' That's true – in love, isn't it?

Please give Gilly a hug & a kiss for me & tell her I miss her. And if she happens to kiss you in return, let it be a railway station kiss from me – on the arrival platform. Frieda darling, be well again.

All my thoughts and love

Alun

214565 Lt A Lewis
GHQ Intelligence School
Old Government House
KARACHI

22nd [August] *Sunday*

Frieda darling,

Are you well again, dearest? Have the tigers gone away & the mountain grown a mole hill and the flowers covered the branch and the grass in the meadows shed its blood-rust and grown green again? Has the trouble gone from your soul, I want to know, leaving only the natural & simple pain of an innocent wound? I've been anxious for you all the week, wondering for you, wishing for you. I'll be glad when you can write to me again. Thank you for choosing my company on Sunday night. Did I suffice? I was listening to music on the lawn till 11 pm – Beethoven's 7th & Dvorak, & thinking of you all the time and being withdrawn into the difficult and remote peaks & ledges of Beethoven's climbing and persistent anguish. Did I suffice?

Today it's again Sunday afternoon, and the post goes at 4. I've had all last night, from 8.30 pm to midnight & all today from 8.30 am to lunch, free to write to you, but I didn't do so. Last night I sat in the dark on the lawn & drank a toast by myself to the spirit I felt moving everywhere then. And then I strolled across to my billet and sat in its bleakness uncertainly, and uncertainly took down one book, then another, then my draft poems then put them all away and read the Bible for two hours. (I read all the life of David.) And in bed I read all the pretty songs in *The Week-End Book*. I get weeks of being like that – uncertain, waiting, groping. I know it's because there's something wishing to take shape in me & write itself. But I can't do anything except lie open to the sky for it & reject the dances & the clubs so that it may have the quiet it desires.

This morning I acted on your instructions with a modicum of efficiency. I narrowed my amber eyes, as you say, to railway time tables and judicious mendacious letters to Adjutants & what nots – & now I am going to produce my PLAN – so you'll have Dick's & mine to make your own out of.

I've written to my regiment asking for four day's leave at the end of my course – (my brother's name is Huw.) If I get it I shall arrive at Bombay (central) at 10.30 am on the 22nd and would be able to stay till the 27th. That's six days and five nights. Now Dick says he can be free for the weekend of the 19th & 20th. So if you left your blue mountains (sounds like Maeterlinck – did Dick tell you how we rang the long bell-pull at Maeterlinck's house at St. Wandrille on the Seine & heard the tinkle it seemed an eternity later deep and faint in the cloisters at dusk?) – if you leave Coonoor on Monday 14th Sept you will be in Poona at 8.30 am on Weds. Sept 16th, see? And you could stay there with Richard Jehu till the 21st or 22nd, & come on to Bombay & meet me. If you left Poona on the 8.30 am (Madras Mail) on the 22nd I could meet you at Bombay V.T. at 12.30 & escort you to the Taj Mahal and all. I've written to the Taj to make a reservation from the 22nd to the 27th. If you'd rather come to Bombay on the 21st and meet *me* you'd better write direct to them, for they're very full – in fact I doubt whether I'll succeed in getting us in there now. I did make a reservation when I passed through on the way here – when I wrote you the note from there – but that was far too early so I've sent them the revised dates & put some kisses on the bottom so they'll oblige please.

Well, is that cut & dried, enough, Daisy Bell? It's awfully soon after your operation for you to be travelling about India in the heat, Frieda, you simply must NOT do it unless you really are recovered. But I'm not hectoring you, you're your own boss. And I don't see any occasion other than this one for us to meet. And I do so earnestly feel we must, you know, must, must, must. Do you mind if I take my shirt off? It is & it isn't your lawn, this one I'm sitting on writing to you. It's hot today. Please come if you can, Frieda darling, I want to be with you, loving you and talking to you, not about Now but about many years, a life time simply.

I slipped down for a bathe this morning after writing all the planning letters & looking up trains & booking a berth at the station. I had a quick bathe & a lot of dives & cycled back with water in my ears to lunch. There were two letters from Gweno & three *Horizons* from her too. I'll send you the *Horizons*, they're very very good. There's a poem by Lynette, the S. American girl with the neurotic surreal husband, remember I told you about her? – and *Horizon* has a lot of things that excite & stir me, like the sight of the little brown robin who used to sit on my books & look in my mirror in the mornings in camp up in the hills by Poona, & defile all my books in the excitement of the image & the mirror. And Gweno's letters had the same effect – a flow of real & closely felt & described experiences which suddenly began flowing through me: and I can't decide whether they are part of me or remain the possession of those who communicate them to me. There's my life, like a little rock, and then suddenly by reading 2 letters and 3 magazines the rock is drenched with a beautiful rain? Is the rain part of the rock? I suppose not. I've growingly had the sensation this last year of the separateness of each one, of the *necessity* for each one to be separate and not try to be identified with someone else. This I mean in terms of personal relations, not political – in politics we must join. But individually, let us be separate, I say. [. . .] And there's an exquisite symphonic rhythm in being separate – in being able to decide within oneself on this stroke, this risk, this refusal, this acceptance – but the *real* music is in being thrillingly & sensitively aware of the separateness of the other one with whom you share love and who is in your arms or in bed with you or five thousand miles away from you. But always you are aware that the beloved is complete, *herself*, & life that just by being itself strikes incessant music out of the silences. And when you do come together, then, God! what music is audible, drowns you, yet is only just audible, beautiful. That's the way I want to love, not this begging and this leaning, but a calm independent love that endures absence and rejoices in meeting, and doesn't destroy or crimp or cripple. I know I'm talking about ideal things, but it's the only thing for which one can strive. You've got it in you, I know. I knew long ago that – never to follow, but always to meet in freedom, the freedom of the will. Oh come & meet me, Frieda.

Everybody is sleeping this afternoon, & arranging for the bearers to bring tea & cream cakes to their rooms. I'm not going to sleep or eat cream cakes today. Fitch. Though I've nothing I want to do except lie awake for this poem, for you, for whatever happens inside me. I do hope you're well now, Frieda darling.

Gweno had a gluttonous time in London – she saw Ibsen's *Ghosts* & *Master Builder*, Turgenev's *Month in the Country*, an Old Vic play called *The Russians*, the International Ballet 'Lac des Cygnes' Amores, Planetomanie – Gawd, what luxury. She saw Philip Unwin who gave her the American edition of *Last Inspection* which she says is unbelievably posh with a smashing dust cover of crossed rifles and cream paper: John Pett's sulky engraving of my head appeared in New York *Herald Tribune* & the book has gone down quite nice & big. She had to give some biographical details to Lilliput, (ha!ha!) for that little Manuel story – and as somebody had made a nasty remark in a review about my social inferiority being responsible for my jibes at the officer class, she wrote me up as a hell of a tough guy. 'Keen boxer & hockey player; revels in battle schools, prefers army to school-mastering.' etc. It's awfully bloody funny, I think. I'm tickled to death with it. She's a bonny girl.

I read an account of Wallace's Rotary lecture in the *Times of India* – I was very pleased to see so friendly a name in the paper. I seem to have cleared out just in time as far as the Governor is concerned, don't I? He sounds the sort that makes me feel awful – the splendid sublimation of the best that is in our Anglo-Indian society – cheap jibe, Alun Lewis – but I'm afraid they make me feel cheap. I can't face them. I don't mind joining a movement to kick them out but I don't want to play at belonging to them. Thank God I've never had to. I've said Tata to Ratan Tata – cheaper joke. Well, I like being cheap; & if you like being expensive, you can be expensive but not in our alley, Sally.

I don't want to finish writing but it's time to post. Thank you for all your letters, Frieda. I wish we were in Bombay today.

Love & kisses
Alun

214565 Lt A Lewis
GHQ Intelligence School
KARACHI

Tuesday 24th

Frieda darling,

This isn't a letter: only a note to thank you for writing so swiftly to let me know you'd survived the operation. I was very very relieved & for a long time didn't want to read the letter because I was so satisfied over the bigger anxiety. I was shy of sending a telegram to you – I hate telegrams at the best of times, they're so fussy & urgent & abrupt – please don't think I was indifferent about it for even an hour of any day till I got your letter. Thank you for it. I'm terribly glad.

This is after lunch – 20 minutes to spare before lectures etc till the mail goes at 4. So it's only a page, not much of a response to your long exciting letter. I'll write tonight, though. I'm very hungry for your letters and they circle round & flow through me all day & in sleep, too. They softly distract me from the lecturer's theme & when I listen to music, as last night, the music is an intensification of – of everything that has become you & ME – you understand. I went up to Toye's room last night & out of a nice library of symphonies etc I chose the Kreutzer Sonata first and then let him play the rest – Mozart & Brahms – because I couldn't listen after the Beethoven to anything.

Frieda, do look after yourself, please. Don't come to Poona & Bombay unless you're really well. But I dream every hour of what we would be doing there – what we *are* doing there, it is – we'd bathe & lie on the lawn in the cricket club where there are hardly any white people except a few R.N. officers & the tiles of the bath are like violets: and buy records in the music shop & argue in the book shop & watch the shipping & the flotsam of the waterfront from the terrace and sing songs from *The Week-End Book* and eat chop suey and dinner-dance with no one to demand of you a dance but me. And loiter on Malabar Hill in the gardens and lie on the beach at Juhu. All these, or none of these, as you choose. And then I think, what if I don't get leave of absence from the 22nd to the 27th – it's very doubtful actually for I've a hint I'll be needed at the unit for a particular business that's afoot – and I have to shut out of my mind as firmly as if I closed a door on somebody all the pure delight of it, and delegate the delight to a category lower than eternity & say O.K. (or Amen, if you prefer). I prefer to say O.K. to big things like fate.

I'm very glad Gilly misses me a little – it gives me a warm feeling very deep in my emotion-world. Your distaste for words comes over me & I never try to speak to you about Gilly because she is – well, just exquisite. Don't worry too much about her school & her luck & her future, Frieda. I've never worried about Mair's because I've known she has all the gifts & all the integrity needed to feel the full terrors and joys that make up the pattern. Gilly won't lack either, as I'm positive she will only grow more & more her beautiful self in them. You too.

This isn't an answer or a letter – it's only a cup of coffee after lunch, or a kiss or a little cloud of sadness passing over the sun.

Solong, darling
Ever
Alun

Frieda darling,

I'm so sorry – I wrote you a little billet at lunch time today in a furious hurry, expressly to bless you for being well again – & in the great rush to post it I didn't post it – & found it in my pigeon hole this evening: so I'll send this by air mail in revenge that it may reach you before the laggard little dove. All the other one had to say was about the loveliness of knowing you were well and not sick or crippled any more. You were sweet to write so long a letter so soon, & to send it by air mail, too: it took 5 days: I could keep on saying how glad I am, but it would tire you. I *am so glad*, Frieda. I worried & worried for you till I heard. And I wouldn't wire you, because wires are all nerves & rush & I was shy also. Words are noisy enough in letters, they beat round me like a flock of big birds, I don't want to put them into telegrams when they are twice as worse! Please get better placidly & gently without bitterness, Frieda. And only come & see me if you really are fit for this naliki-naliki, never never train. In Bombay you can rest & rest for the little heaven that lasts – I dream incessantly of what we can do – will you be fit to swim with me in the lawn blue baths in the Cricket club & have Samora & ice for tea, and a handful of delights I know? Oh I hope you will. I hope my battalion lets me go. I hope hope hope. I'll know by a week today & will wire you their answer No or Yes, so you'll know what to decide about Mrs Aykroyd's September guests.

I came here for quiet & the little captain who sleeps next to me didn't go to the Club but came here to undress, drop things & prattle & croon tonight so I've got to close both ears.

There are so many things in your letters that I don't specifically answer, but I read and 'know' what you say in the way you want me to, Frieda. And I am always coming to you & being with you, darling, and never going away from you, never, never, not even in the dark lane in the wood when I felt the barren rock cry out with its terrible invincible hardness in the open heart I had. You say things about my poems & stories that I do not expressly answer, either, because I am content with your saying them simply. Mostly I let the things I've written pass away from me. If they have merit I don't want it for myself. If they are like radium, emanating a little glow of themselves, then I'm glad, but I don't take it upon myself. The only thing I respect in myself are the poems & stories I haven't yet written. These I work for with all the power I can gather, fiercely as any mother. I don't worry even what other people are writing, the new tricks, the modernism; I read them with pleasure & a thrill of something new & exciting, but I don't try to be like them or like anything or anybody, in the same way as I've never tried to meet any of these people, preferring to go my own way & be that hardest of things, my-self. Nobody & nothing has succeeded in preventing me, not even myself, though many powerful beings have tried, often not intentionally. The sensitiveness to criticism or the desire for praise you speak of is very real, it's fundamental really, yet it's only the word from the very *near* person that one wants, to be fertilised thereby: the critic's opinion is a pale thing with no more warmth to warm or burn than the moon has. But mother's quiet support was everything I needed, & daddy's inarticulateness was like a shadow all over me so that I avoided him: it's the same as you say. Except that one does go on & on, praise or no praise. I love your 17 year old poem – 'To suffer, suffer, yet to feel no pain' – it's very moving and clear as tears are: you grew old very early, didn't you? Marrying when I couldn't have dreamed of being bedded, having a child when all I wanted was the spirit of existence & I choked & got drunk & cut all sorts of capers because it was not in me, and now Peter & Gilly so manifest and complete – I haven't really tried to understand all this in you, and – it's only a few days, odd, just a few days – I've never needed to because it was before the last 15 years began that I met you in Coonoor and perhaps you were sixteen when you hid your face, smiling & hiding your face by the lakeside. And I thought no more than a peasant does, life being one thing & knowing the centre of it there.

But you mustn't worry about Dick or tell him to hate or how to dislike what – Dick's alright, don't try to alter that boy. He's 12 stone of his sweet self & I think he can hand it out to whoever deserves it. He doesn't go wrong much. You touched me saying he was hurt because you didn't like *Raiders' Dawn*. Bless him – I didn't know I had such a bully champion. I thought Mair was my only chivalrous banneret, & she's far too modest & proud to speak of such things. When I met Dick in Poona last February for the first time I was surprised how he was still 'outside' India; I thought he'd have become it, being with Indian troops. I know I'm miles & miles outside it, not as far as an ICS, but hopelessly far for a poet to be. My chief salvation is the awareness of this, and the strange feeling that comes sometimes, & swings me into an immediate & brief communion with this country. I think the spade work of learning the language, & reading books on the tribes & districts & the clarity to use your eyes all the time & see, see, see – all of them help: & reading the Upanishads: but I know I'm miserably alien to much of all this – its forts & temples I shall never grow fond of & never want to. But I do love its villages & could share their life without loss. I'm careful not to write from the outside moods. So I write little. 'The Orange Grove' was deep inside; just for those two nights I was possessed by the journey I'd made in the Jeep & there was nothing else under the sun but that compulsion.

But what is all this? Writing about writing again! Shucks.

I wrote a poem last night. I wonder what it's like. Also I listened to the Kreutzer Sonata, Hugh Toye asked me up to his room & told me choose my records – so it was your records I must choose. It moved & intensified me moult bien. I can listen & listen to it & it's always new, always another depth or delight or doubt or illumination. Also I found the record Lynette Roberts sent me once – 'Una Furtiva Lacrima' – Donizetti – Gigli sings it to a harp obbligato – God it's so good. I tried to buy you one but Karachi lacks it.

I want to talk to you about some things, not write of them at all. One huge thing happened to me on Monday night when I was all alone – I sang it to myself, the thing that happened; the room was empty & I was naked splashing water over myself & singing this enormous & dreadful joy that came up to me so casually & said something quite final & terrible to me & I laughed and sang it back. It was in my sleep, too, & when I woke, yesterday morning & this morning, and I'm delighted that I can sing it & not shudder over it. I'll tell you this, perhaps, if it's still in me in September in Bombay. Hurry up, old churlish time. Please will you.

I've still not seen Karachi; I've not been to a cinema or cafe or anywhere except to swim & watch the camels crossing the railway bridge, & the green river & the sour green sea holly flats by the swimming jetty. Dhows from Arabia & Africa & Cochin cluster down there. I love their yards & masts & piled ropes. Otherwise I drink a gimlet in the darkness & write to you & to scarcely anyone else. The School is throwing a dance on Friday night and a chap called Poole said would I escort a nurse who wanted to come with his woman & I said 'I'm not bothered' so I'm going to escort this here nurse on Friday, & not having seen her before I don't really want to very much. Still Friday is only another Friday.

Oh I wish I could have some more of these pellucid days.

Goodnight, Frieda: you know my thoughts couldn't be gentler, darling.

XXXXXXXXXX

X   Love   X

XXXXXXXXXX

Alun

214565 Lt. A Lewis
GHQ Intelligence School
KARACHI

Thursday, Aug 26th

Frieda darling,

I get a particular little joy in putting the 'i' in Frieda now, and having done it wonder why I've been shy of writing to you for two days. I've missed you for two days, had the sinking sensation of twice looking vainly for letters from you, and thinking about you not twice but steadily, with a steadiness that I have to respect, as if I bowed before a better man – and I've avoided writing to you. Now that I do write, some of the inhibition falls away. Some remains. I'm afraid of writing out of this queer emptiness that is among the planets. Two evenings ago a genuine mood of poetry came over me, while I was swimming & cycling back – but I missed the reality & got caught among the word snags – and so gradually came a hardening, a growing suspicion of the nothingness that was succeeding the poesie manquée. And I wouldn't write to you out of it, but chose to surround it with my self. I don't know why I'm telling you about it now. It's against the code of pride; but it's better than the insincerity of hiding. During the last two nights I have talked to two men I like very much, Hugh Toye and Michael Clark, two civilised and softly spoken creatures who *think & live* all the time as best they can, & take the trouble to worry & buy books & records, and consider people as souls rather than colonels or decent chaps. Michael is suffering from an undiagnosed disease and some mental despair I don't understand yet, & I've got a powerful feeling I can help him a bit. He's a tank instructor, on the staff here. I've hardly met him. Hugh Toye is an instructor too, very dainty of mind, with a huge spotted hound, a piano, & a craze for flying. I talked very well with them, hiding this emptiness completely: in a way it's easier to talk then, because one is so disinterested and has no personal sensations & can see more easily the conflict of all points of view, & the pre-eminence of none. You know all this, Frieda, and I know & you know how it would go just with us being together. 'But we're not together' says the emptiness with icy lucidity of his marble voice. Quite, says the echo, oh quite, you old bastard. In the same mood I was called upon out of a daydream by the chief instructor yesterday to criticise the student speaker of the day – we have a routine talk on current affairs & a routine criticism each day – & I got up & with this coldness proceeded to criticise the boy who'd been speaking about the Quebec conference on Anglo-Russian relations & the India famine. When I'd finished I sat down. And everybody clapped. I was astounded. And lots of them said something about it since – about 'honesty' 'gravity' 'sincerity' – it's all really very very odd, because the kernel of it was this emptiness of the personality, and the way one is open then to the eternal factors of human life. The war comes uppermost. The self, & love, & all warm nearnesses recede. But truly I hadn't realised all the time that I was speaking that I was saying anything – I seemed to be fighting with hard words and powerful ideas & it was difficult to choose the real words.

Frieda darling, I must go to bed; I'm keeping the other two from sleeping, the light breaks through their mosquito nets. Goodnight, Frieda darling, you must be gentle and not blame me for being all the things that happen to happen. Goodnight, kamerade, liebste.

And yet I don't want to sleep. I want to get beyond this poverty of the imagination. I know there is a way – and intuition says the way is through Burma. Maybe it isn't, maybe that's only the bait on the trap. But I've listened this week three nights to music – the Kreutzer sonata on Monday, Brahms' 2nd piano concerto on Wednesday, Chaikovsky's 6th tonight: I thought of you to the exclusion of people and past & future: and I nearly attained that sudden capacity to speak with the tongue of angels: but no, back to the start again, to the sixteenth, seventeenth, twenty-second year, when there was nothing to be said, nothing. I don't mind really, I've got to wait, & time doesn't matter in this. Only just this midnight, in this bare room, the mosquitoes on my bare shoulders that the sun has tanned and enriched with pimples, just for this Now, I feel sad at it all. I've got another friend who's got a face just like Mephistopheles, very distinguished satanic features, & who's killed a lot of Japs off & on, I'm going to the races with him on Saturday. It's very funny, but I don't feel like laughing one bit.

Thank you for your love letters, Frieda. I could come to you now, I know, like this, and you'd let me come and you'd still me. I had a wonderful feeling of the certainty of that this afternoon in the middle of a lecture by the C.I.D. man. It made my heart beat, the sudden involuntary accession of knowledge in my heart. I will need you very much, you know, very very much. The greater part of 'Fate' is attraction, isn't it, the machination of a force like a subterranean river. Attraction. Fate. Fate. Attraction. How deeply I am aware of you *now, now*. To the bitter end is also a phrase.

Outside the wind is in the bushes, sifting and winnowing the warm darkness, piling it up in soft clouds of chaff. Inside the scratching of my pen like the scratching of the gramophone needle over all that is in Beethoven. These little sounds are very friendly & kind, the wind, the needle, the scratching of mice. In a larger mood the voices of children & Indian sweepers, and even men. But tonight I want only the sigh of the wind. And now not even that, but sleep & you to come to me in sleep, in the not knowing parts of us, and the broken poem to mend itself quietly by itself in the space we can give it. And peace in your arms, oh please bring your peace.

Goodnight, Frieda, your dark hair & your gold and your regrets & your vitality. Come soon, quietly. One morning you woke me.

Friday morning: 8.15 am

Now you must bundle me off before school, in good time you know, woollen muffler, stockings pulled up over pink knees if there are hailstones, little Dai-cap down over untidy cow's lick hair – that's how mother used to send me off – & when I was teaching in Pengam she'd be just the same, in the kitchen in her dressing gown making hot toast and tea & cutting sandwiches for my attaché case with all the textbooks or boys' essays marked in blue lead & a book of poems for the train, dark winter mornings when the dead ashes in the grate are so frozen-looking. Here the Indians make our breakfasts & we are the top caste in the Hindu tree and toy with our sacrilegious bacon and our holy eggs.

Lunch: and now another five minutes before the afternoon starts. Darling, I've just had your letter air mail of the 18th. Nine days, it's taken. Quel allegresse!

You found it a hard letter to write. I'm glad. Horrible Kafka Brigadier. You lunch with such Bulgarian atrocities, Frieda, don't you?

I can't 'answer' your letter now – can't talk of aloneness and one-ness here, in a five minutes after coffee rush. Bless you.

Dick wrote a little note, too. Neither here nor there. *You* must receive all his letters now – I used to get such a lot once.

People are everywhere, in the next chair & talking against my knees. This idiot dance is tonight. Tomorrow evening I'm going to have a chop suey with Michael Clark. Are you going to meet me in Bombay, I wonder? Everything revolves round that now. I was very 'digalon' last night – do you know 'digalon' now? Something like the blues in negro american – but not Charing X Road blues at all. Vast empty blues. A hard tin cylinder with dry peas in it enters the composition, also.

I must finish, Frieda. You've had my letters that answer yours, now, haven't you? They don't answer either. I'm afraid not. But they're my straight undeluding response to them. That's all I can give you.

Thank you for sending the books.

Love to Gilly

Come on, let's hurry

XX

XX

Alun

Frieda darling,
And now I am surrounded by so many lovely evidences of you. Zola
& Voltaire & Huxley on the chest by my side, and on the arm of
this army-type chair the two letters you wrote to me on Tuesday,
one in the lab. in the morning & one with bread and honey in the
afternoon, and the four photographs that make me ache so in my
bones & nerves & flesh with the recognition and delight of *looking*
at you, & looking at Gilly, and saying Hallo so happily to Wallace
& Col. Purvis and returning as I always did in their company to
the secret river-like contemplation of you, you, you. Oh Frieda do
you know how deeply you have pierced in me? How everywhere
you have restated, revived, broken down and compelled in me,
so that, as I gradually encounter the beliefs I had, I find one after
another is changed, maybe replaced, maybe just lost & nothing yet
in its place? And now I am hunger & thirst and effort and this
strange intense joy that really is pain as well as joy, not because it is
complex but because it is commensurate with life, and with all
that the imagination has ever explored and identified and known.
And your restless desire to know I'd received your letters is like my
anxiety to know you'd received *my* reply to *your* letters: that the
chain be complete, 'that the night come'. You know & I know that we
are forging armour together, making ourselves, seeking while there
is time for the strength of understanding, and being strong enough
to wait, to lack, to speak, to be silent, to endure. And these letters
we send, often they bring joy suddenly, like an English sunshower,
or the serious and grave reply that everything aches for, they are

doing so much. You've done so terribly terribly much today, now, this afternoon, with these two letters, these four photographs, to me. I've been having a bad time, darling, just a bad time. At noon today I didn't know where to turn from it; I didn't want to look at lunch but made myself go & eat it & talk to the 'chaps' – and came soberly away with your letters to somewhere alone: & oh God it's so wonderful. Sunday afternoon I know what you are all doing – and now it isn't difficult to find you and take you for a walk in the woods. And you will come to Bombay? Can you? Yes you say yes yes yes and I incredulously keep on saying can you?, because it is somehow a physical miracle. And the sight and sound of you so holy to my wondering and worshipping hands & eyes. Darling Frieda, I'm very old in my familiarity with hurt & hardness: I pray that you are also. We will love most best through a bravery shared and not spoken of again by me, ever, ever. Joy is manifestly a thing that comes & goes. We need it and love it, but I never will try & hold it: it hurts too badly to hold it against its will, and perhaps what you & I will need most is bravery. I can't explain; I only know we'll have to hang on to *nothing* for long tracts of time, Frieda, and that it is imperishable – *this*.

Darling, don't let yourself think of me as a little youth. Nor as a poet nor as a writer. I am something much harder, more obstinate and vulnerable and devoted and blindly determined than any of these people. I am just an instinct when it becomes real and there are no embellishments. It is that instinct I want to give to you, I want you to feel inside you, knowing you in the first element of all & the last element of all and all the time before now & now and ever after now.

This weekend I've peeled away the poet & the boy & the uniform and the intelligence officer and the particular lover. Michael Clark made me do it. He's a gentle intensely humane & cynical & faith-keeping man and if there are any lies they fall off like a snake's old skin. Darling, last night we cleared out of the School & the Club & the faces & went to a chop suey house downtown and in the hot little room eating steaming unpleasant omelettes among the Americans & sergeants & their fast chichi girls I showed him some poems. The ones I'm putting in this letter, and also 'Ways', 'The Field', 'The Wood', and 'Beloved Beware'. Without context, without a word, just as poems you know. And he said '"The Journey" is good: possibly the "Gateway of India". The others are facile, aren't they? One of them is nice ("The Field"), I think'. He said 'facile': it hurt like hell & bloody hell, and he realised it & we were very disjointed after that. There was nothing facile about that bitter day in the empty room in Ratan Tata, or the black night before when I tried so hopelessly to find words. Nor in the cycle I hired and rode away away & the hills I climbed in the mist. It *wasn't* facile, Christ it wasn't. Michael, why did you say that?

And yet it is true that I cannot write you the poetry that is yours until long after this is over and it is part of me & I have made myself see the world again with my new eyes that you said were blind, as of course they are, as a newborn animal's are. The rest of the night was unbearable though we sat on the terrace until 1 a.m. & he talked about the big tank battle where he began his head trouble. He has fought a lot – at Sidi Rezegh & Knightsbridge, the Cauldron; the withdrawal to El Alamein was when he caught it for the last time, his tank exploded under a direct hit & his wireless operator from the Rhondda crawled a mile alongside him without any legs and then Michael had to leave him and cannot forget his piteous eyes at being left alone. And the rest of the crew blown to bits & burnt out. He's had a string of cerebral operations with the shrapnel inside his head, and he is a very beautiful person. I want you to meet him and I've talked for the first time to anybody just odd little bits of talk about Wallace's work and Gilly's poems and sometimes for the secret delight of saying your name I've quoted something you said to me, but I've carefully said nothing else. I'm very jealous of anyone divining - - - - - - I - - - - - -

But of course I can't write the real real real poems yet. A very big thing happens & after it, under its impact, one is for a long time apparently smaller. Like concussion. Through the window bars the yellow bungalow across the way has rambling bougainvillaea. I know it will be alright ultimately. But you also must promise not to be hurt in any wrong way, by any seeming meanness & failure in me. Take me for all in all, I am a man. I can dare to say that. I can just dare to say that.

Frieda, I think I'll be in Bombay on the 21st, not the 22nd. Will you come on 21st if that is so? That's on the Tuesday? A whole new day given us. But I must not think, – not until I hear from Gwyn to know whether they're releasing me or not. I'll wire you as soon as I hear. It's not very far away now.

I've messed things up a bit here with that critique I told you about – I've got to give an hour's lecture to see whether I'm fit to be an instructor here – ugggggh. But I'm telling them quite definitely that even if I were good enough I wouldn't bloody lecture until I'd been to Burma. And I won't. Not at any price. After that I'd love to. It would be natural then. Now it would be presumption and I *won't* do it.

The dance last Friday was surprisingly pleasant. The nurse I fetched & partnered & returned to the fold was a good looking Northumberland maiden who has only been in India for 10 days & she was quite different from the flotsam of the club who were also present. None of the wizened felinity with which they watch the goings on. She had heat bumps and bug bites on her legs and was quite disarmingly natural & simple. I hadn't expected anyone to whom one could chatter and be easy & unarmed. I wonder whether India will alter her & whether she'll ever notice what is happening to her & how it is making her ugly.

I must catch the post now – I must write to Dick & Huw too, later. Oh I wish I could write the poems now, darling, it would be such a relief.

I love you & cannot bear to say so except with my voice to you.

Auf Wiedersehen,
Alun

P.S. *Darling, darling,*
darling, darling, darling,
darling, darling, darling,
darling Frieda.

214565 Lt. A. Lewis
GHQ Intelligence School
KARACHI

Tuesday August 31ˢᵗ
Late at night

Frieda Darling,

It is like the settlement of a disorder to turn at last like this with pen & paper, and lay aside the work and the mind's divisions and do nothing with this Now but surrender myself to this act of writing.

I haven't had a letter from you today, nor yesterday and all the time the malaise has grown and I'm sick of it hammering away, hammering, hammering. I need your real presence & that is all I need. Otherwise I ache only for oblivion, the desert, fighting & the laughter of a spirit grappling with brutality. All bad things: it's ugly, this silken fascination that evil has some times. Writing of it releases me from it.

Thank you very very much for the four photographs, Frieda. They are most dear to me and give me such pleasure and peace and closeness. I do love your Gilly. And as for you, I gaze & gaze and am quietly and blessedly happy. Michael's niece, three years Gilly's senior, was being prepared for confirmation at a girl's boarding school in England & wrote home her profound doubts thus: 'The whole business of the immaculate conception seems to me to smack of the extremely improbable'. Is that one worse than the two pigeons – the sage of 11 or the saint of seven? Is Gilly seven? Sweet Gilly.

I'm in the dead middle of nowhere this week. A big American (Joseph Crew?) said the Jap war will go on to 1949. It's weighed me down, although I've always thought so. I can never stick that long – the laws of probability reject such a long immunity. The RAF go home at the end of three years if they're married, four if they're single. Darling, I haven't heard from the Regiment yet: I'm seriously afraid I won't get any leave on the 21st. I was doubtful all the time for I knew there was some agenda on the minutes (?what?) – circumlocution gone wrong – if I don't hear tomorrow I'll be really despondent. Will you still go to Poona & see Dick? I could probably be free for a *day* but no more. Oh God – but why be miserable before I have proof of misery? But there is timelessness as well as time, and I find myself moving more easily every day between the two planes. 'If we shall meet again why we shall laugh – ' And I know we will.

I had a copy of a Lehmann anthology called New Writing & Daylight today with a massive collection of good writing in it by all sorts of distinguished people. It had a poem of mine in, a long one called 'Embarkation' which I typed out the last day I was home – remember I told you how I spent the last day typing, & Gweno was so good, she never upbraided me at all. (She wished it to appear like the middle day in a steady lifetime.) I was surprised at its general quality – I hadn't read it all before & it's quite good. I'm quite proud of it. [. . .] I hope I can bring the book down with me, but at the moment it's been STOLEN – some bloody thief took it from my pigeon-hole where I put it at lunch after nothing but a glance at it, too. And Gweno paid 30/– to send it here by air mail. I feel so sick at losing it. God knows whether it'll ever be returned. It maybe somebody wanted to sell it down town – or it may be just a high-brow pickpocket.

Frieda, I must try and write to you of the trouble in me. It will be harder to write of later if I keep silent now, although something prompts me to keep silent. Not a word I say has any hurt or hate in it, darling, nor does it detract a grain from all my love. And you will understand that I am only speaking one-sidedly because I wouldn't presume to preach or assume anything for you.

May I speak to you, darling? Listen then. I'm speaking very quietly, as you know when it's hard to speak.

I love Gweno very deeply. I can feel her love all the time, its reality and its deep tides. She worked miracles for me, not once but many times. There were terrible nightmares & sterilities in me & sometimes I got unbearably lost & parched & stunned in them, & frightened so that I cried & cried & cried, cried my heart out: and then she was always strong enough to make the terrible journey herself. Sometimes it was a real journey, by train: sometimes it was in bed, whether before we married or after. It would be impossible for me not to love her.

When I came to Coonoor, Frieda, I had a tremendous vivid premonition, like a birth in the spirit; all the time I drew nearer this exultation grew and when at last the taxi took me from the station to Highfield I was incandescent it was marvellous. And yet it had no positive point, no physical purpose, no foresight or expectation. It wasn't conscious thought. I never *thought*, darling, never, never, never. When at last at midnight you called me, when I was sitting away from you & the other two men, tired with the journey & the drink in a thoughtless void, & I heard you say my name to me & I got up & came & sat by you, then, suddenly, out of that void of weariness and landlessness, I *knew*. I can't write that word 'knew' strongly enough. I'm not imagining any of this that I'm writing.

From the moment I put my left arm around your neck and touched your shoulder and drew your lovely head down to me and my lips lay in your hair I loved you, darling and love you love you love you. And want you so much and have known you for so long that we are always going back farther & farther & farther into the heart of things.

The trouble is in the conflict of two tides of loving. I hoped devoutly there need be no conflict; perhaps later there won't be, perhaps my being will grow enough to understand the existence of things: but now it's trouble in me, trouble in the mind & in the body, and I don't know, I just don't know, darling. Do you know? Can you tell me? I'm so weary with wanting your hands & lips and aloneness. I'm so worthless, too, beloved. You have asked me to be careful of our love. Love is one of the few things we can't be careful about. It lives & dies in its own nature. Care can not foster it, nor lack of care kill it. All it asks is honesty. That is all I'm trying to give. Honesty and love.

[...]

Frieda, I'm not asking you for advice or to do anything. I only want you to know. If you know it will be infinitely happier for me. I can love you if you know how I am made. Perhaps there is nothing new in this to you. I think of you saying Yes, you knew it all. Does it alter anything? Will you still come, and will you know that the love I give you is true love?

I won't write any more, darling. I don't know what else to write about.

Nothing else matters.

Goodnight lovely Frieda my darling

Ever & ever
Alun

Frieda darling,

I sent you a wire at lunch time to let you know my pessimism was unjustified by the event, and that I'm free as the wild wind from the 21st to the 27th after all. I received a telegram from the Battalion saying 'Leave Granted: Writing' – I don't think the latter will contain any stipulations: anyway I'm not thinking of objections any more or what might go wrong: I'm just going to think of you until you *are* you. Will you come on Tuesday – or whatever the 21st is? I've cabled the Taj Mahal saying we're arriving on Tuesday.

Will you wear my name, darling? It's not a very nice one, but will you accept it? It'll be a young name, a few days old, but it won't be smelling of new paint but of new flowers only. Please will you be my name? I wish it were Kashmir: I can rejoice in a sophisticated city, but there is never the same tranquil and unrestricted enlargement of spirit in a city as in hills or rivers. 'Again', tolls the pretty bell across the fields, 'another time, again'. And all the cattle bells say 'Next Time, Next Time', and the camel bells say 'What?'. I wish it were Provence, Bavaria, Chamonix, the French Alps, an outer island of a coast of islands. Think, there are no more tourists in those lovely places. Everyone is at the war, as if they're at the races, and there are only the places there, being themselves. I'm sending you three *Horizons* for the journey. Dick will gobble them up at Poona, so he can have them for *his* journey also. Will you listen to my poems and the stutter in the middle – they're on Sunday night (12th) at 8.30, I think – or 8.45.

Thomas in my room here has just given me – guess – a penny! A dear black Victorian penny. Has Gilly got one in her box? I'm going out to see Michael at the hospital – he's got ear trouble and a temperature – he isn't really well at all. And then I've promised to have supper at the club. Tomorrow night I'm out on an all night exercise so I won't be able to write to you till Sunday. And for some reason I can't write much tonight, darling. I don't want to talk or write but just to lie still somewhere open and fresh and listen to music or feel you near. I turned away from the offer of a captaincy and a staff job yesterday although it was a real active job. I don't want to leave my battalion yet. Something very sad and unargumentative keeps me part of it. I won't leave it. But that job was a temptation. If I was reasonable – but no, it's obvious. I can't do any job till I've been in action and come out of it. All else is cowardice and inferior and would be shameful to me.

If a letter comes from you tomorrow I will be able to take it with me on this exercise & sleep with it in the desert. I hope one comes.

Frieda darling, I'm so relieved that there will be freedom that I'm unnaturally serious, as one is after a narrow escape.

Good night, darling
All love
Alun

Friday, after lunch
Before I pop this into the letter box, just a tiny salutation from the middle of an empty day. Hello, Frieda, do you feel like going out in the back of a truck and making a reconnaissance of a square mile of desert? Must do it today: but a fortnight today I won't do it. What shall we do after lunch a fortnight today?

No letter from you today either. I'm a bit anxious for you, & wish I could hear. I'm wondering whether Madras was too much for you, but I won't think spinsterish old things like that. I'm waiting for Lloyds Bank to tell me they've transferred some money from my flowing bowl at home. I asked them five weeks ago & if it doesn't come soon I'll be in a considerable spot.

I had two disquieting letters from Gweno today: she's living in a sort of hourly anxiety, it's such a deadly drain on her spirit, & she must somehow push those black fears back into the sub sub sub conscious & lock them up, like a funeral dress. To wear them daily isn't right at all: and to so empty herself of everything but love: it disturbs me very deeply. And yet I know that I can't help her & that it is her own task entirely. It is in fact her *self*.

I'm very impatient of the hours I spend in school here. I chafe against the superfluities and irrelevances & desire to write and can't. I don't even read, so 'bitty' is everything. I shall be glad to be rid of it, and back to the solid realities of troops & guns and marches & blisters & sweat & action. I can write there because I live in a spiritual tranquillity and clarity more than I can here. I wrote 'Orange Grove' in a spiritual Parnassus in the centre of a physical hurly burly. I love it when it's like that – it's a thrilling synthesis of living & writing, thought & deed, wrong & right. It's like being in love.

Frieda darling, I must go now – can you hear the rooks & the pies & squirrels & the wind in the evergreens?

Come soon, time
My love
Alun

124

Frieda darling,

It's 10.20 p.m. Saturday night and I'm very lucky. I've got no one spending the weekend with me and I'm alone, alone, and Time passes. I'm very happy, and as you say, rich as Croesus. Tonight I'm alone here & very happy. This is how it is.

I went out yesterday on this exercise affair and slept on a cliff top with a great white surf thundering below like a masculine angel. I couldn't sleep. I sat for an hour in your company on the brink of the cliff, looking at great starry scorpio curling his tail over the south and letting the sea reverberate through me, thinking 'Penbryn is sea & cliff, & this sound. This sound is deep & familiar in me. I am not sitting alone on a desert shore by a sea called the Arab in longitude 72, latitude 29 1/2: I am at home, the world is filling me with its sounds. I'm very happy & near to love, warm with love, cherished by this sweetness, this overwhelming sweet sound. Then I stripped and climbed into my sheet and nearly slept. But my mind started thinking about work and for hours I turned over the problems of the exercise and odd jobs outstanding, such as the propaganda poster or blurb we've got to write or compose & which I abominate & abhor. And the Brains Trust on combined operations which I've got to stage next Thursday. So that when I put my head under the sheet & cupped my hand round my watch to illuminate the dial it was 1.30 – & I'd been lying there since 10. I felt lonely & hard then, thinking of work, 'school work', tedious self-stopping work: and then I must have slept. When I woke the greyness of first light dazzled my eyes. I had piles of work to do, piles, piles, piles, walking, wading, measuring, judging, making notes & sketch-maps, little busybody writing up a report. I finally finished the whole job & put my file in the major's box at 7.15 this evening. The sun was strong out there and I slipped my shirt off and got tanned & licked by the great doggy tongue of the sun and all the time my mind was very cool & lucid and I controlled the work of my syndicate like an old hand. But when I strolled back here I was quite flat. And I sat and looked at my mail. One from Frieda. One from Becky, Howell's wife, who is very beautiful and sparkly & bright in life and writes such boring letters always. One from Mother, from Penbryn. One from Gweno from Aberystwyth. I read Frieda's.

I read it in the flatness I was in, eager to break through the flatness into all the other dimensions of love & life. But I read it only to see that you weren't ill – it's so long since I heard from you & I was worried for you – and just to see what you said. Then I put some water in the bath & lay in it, soaking my salty, sandy hair, & careful not to wet my hands, read your letter again. Slowly & peacefully, in the tranquillity of any day I was with you, the rare thing it is.

And your words lapped & flowed round my hot sunny flatness and everything you wrote was like your voice beside me, oh very close & near and loving, and it explained and I replied, sometimes only with a kiss, & sometimes with the silence of gratitude or simplicity or sorrow, & sometimes urgently at a big misunderstanding. It was a lovely letter, it went through & through me. Thank you & bless you, Frieda. I want it to be just as you want it; only I'm not as clear & inwardly mature as you & I have conflicts you have outgrown. And sometimes I oversay a thing, exuberantly, and you read it as meaning something too much. That remark I made about feeling a 'hell of a guy' – I shouldn't have said that because it wasn't how I felt. Not quite. I was trying to say that one plays the world at its own game in certain places. In a club one goes in and accepts certain of the club's principles & values. And I just knew I was the most favoured 'partner' in the Coonoor Club, you see; but I had a sort of silent laugh at the cats & the dogs. Although I prefer not to enter their bedlam at all, I like winning the race when I'm an outsider. In just the same way as occasionally I've enjoyed telling a man to his face, in pub or club or changing room of a rugger team, and asking him with an insolent eye whether he'd like to fight it out. It's only devilment: you've got lots. That's all I was saying, Frieda Buttery.

But that's too flamboyant a world to live with – it's never more than a caprice. And darling Frieda, how much more more I answer your words 'how much I am humble in loving, All my loving. In being alive at all.' Oh Frieda, Frieda, Frieda. And I'm humble, so much so that it unbalances me. Sometimes I have to stop myself grovelling before awful loud bullying colonels and whatnots because their assumption of absolutism suddenly hits me where I am truly humble and I cave in. Other times, & most times nowadays, it makes me stand up and say my mind to those people. As I did yesterday in the school – it's like a parliament – a conservative parliament. A colonel was talking on China – & at the end I got up & went for him. I knew I was cooking my military goose & I sat down & felt a sort of hollowness, anticlimax, & the commandant smoothed my challenge aside with 'That's a big question, but it's *politics*. This is a *military* school'. Neat convenient compartments all designed to maintain the old abuses & wrongs, the deep bitter blood-demanding wrongs which we suffer & suffer & by suffering them insult & degrade the humanity that we are. Frieda, I will treasure these five days that are coming, treasure them now in my heart in my cupped hands. Good days, kind days, love days, thought days, undeserved gentleness of days. I will take you with me everywhere. X (A kiss is put here.)

It's midnight now. Thomas came in at the bottom of the last page and said 'Come & have a nightcap at the club'. So I said O.K. They were all dancing and drinking. I'd been five months in India before I went to a club. Then I looked inside the Poona Club & saw all the white women and thought 'So this is where they live & have their being'! As if I'd discovered the nesting habits of a rare bird or the propitious climate of a delicate insect. Anyway, there they were tonight.

Frieda, I'm dreadfully sorry I couldn't understand your letters about the operation. Darling, it would be so terrible for you, but I *couldn't* come near enough then. Something seemed to say 'Keep away, keep away', like a stolid unimaginative policeman 'It's not your concern, mister. Keep away'. So I just hated it & hated it and couldn't understand. I did try to darling, and I have done since, but I failed you then. I'm sorry sorry sorry. Don't be grieved, Frieda darling. I can help you not to grieve, I believe I can. Stroking your hair like this, now.

Thank you for lots of definite solid things, for the books & the photographs & the solid envelopes & paper & handwriting of your letters that are so powerful to me & make a cyclone about themselves & thrill me when I pick them up. Thank you also for what Jerry said of 'Bread and Stones', and the man in the club of *Last Inspection*. It does please me, but I don't *need* it from others. I need what you yourself think. Thank you indeed for that too. What others think is important to me because I want to win their ear, their interest, even their tacit approval, for the time when there will be something practical & urgent to say. 1950? 1951? Will I still care? Will I be alive? I think of that curiously. You say something of yourself – Tod und die Mädchen – that moves me massively & makes me deny it wildly & possessively for you against Death & take you to Kashmir or Vezelay where HE can't come. But darling, are you also within the charmed circle? And isn't it in some ways very beautiful? To accept just whatever it will be. But we will *not* accept, Frieda. Neither Frieda nor Alun, do you hear, you two children? Can you bring 'Bread & Stones' with you, Frieda? I haven't read it yet. I'm very pleased Jerry liked it, he's a man of quality. Will you tell me your address in Poona? No, no need. I'll write to you c/o Dick. Will you dance with me? Swim with me? Loll on the balcony over the shipping with me? Will you *please* bring Rilke with you, please please please bring Rilke with you to read in the early night & perhaps one pellucid morning? Are you going to stay in Poona afterwards? I won't get much time off – one day in ten – we're a long way out of Poona & come in by truck. If I returned there on the Sunday (27th) I wouldn't probably get into Poona till the following Saturday night or Sunday. C'est à toi de décider, bien aimée. Frieda, come to bed with me. It's a small bed, Darling XXXXX

XXX

Alun

Sunday morning

It's a morning like a story of Katherine Mansfield, vrai et vivace et bel. I think it will become insufferably hot later, but now there is a vigorous cool wind and the excited singing & cawing of birds. A fortnight today I'll be in Lahore, waiting all day for the Frontier Mail. Soon, soon now.

I slept badly last night. I was nearly asleep when the third member of the room came in, un peu soûlé, with an American captain in the same state & proceeded to make a bed for our ally on the floor. I lay awake till between 3.30 & 4, listening to the snores, with nothing in my head at all all the time, & sometimes I sighed long & loud & luxurious, deflating myself further. Now it's this morning and I still feel the emptiness of last night but all the day is ready to brim into it over its miserable little groyne.

After I'd read your letter last evening I read Becky's & mother's & Gweno's. Mother describing the beach & the mill cottage where we stay & the pair of seals who have lived in the camel rocks since we were kiddies, and her M.D. sister who came down to rest her broken mind & made the week outrageous & horrible with her evil talk, and Mair in her bathing scanties brown & vital & puzzled by Auntie Ray & avoiding her. And Gweno's letter full of the two little children, her nephew William Edward the blond piglet, and redheaded Lou whose daddy is a prisoner in Japan. Gweno mothers them every holiday – she loves to bed them & sing German lieder to them till she can smell 'the smell of children's sleep', as she says. Then she took them up the hill past Jack Price's donkeys & over to Cwm Woods where the silver birches twist like heraldic serpents & the broad Llangorwen valley is yellow with mustard seed & irises in the marsh & the sea sounds softly all up the valley. I know it so well, it's like peace to read her words. Then a little Indian editor of a poetry magazine has lost some of my poems. He's a bounder, anyway, a sham. Then she thinks she'll go & work in Robert Herring's office after the war, if I get a job in London, & help him to edit Life & Letters because he isn't as erratic and peculiar-feeling as Connolly & all the other 'literary' boys. Although she'd prefer to live in a cowshed somewhere and have Shan and Nevin.

There's a fat dove strutting across the lawn by the bougainvillaea. I wish I could be strolling with you looking at the rose moles all in stipple in your little stream. And the gardeners in white are coming to weed.

I hope the *Horizons* reach you in time, Frieda. I posted them on Friday, three of them. You will like them. Today I must go and see Michael in hospital and I'm having tea with Geoffrey Pitchford, a private soldier in my regiment who is doing a course up here, and tonight I'll listen to music perhaps. Maybe a bathe & some school-work also. No writing of poems today.

I won't write to Highfield again this week. I'll write to you to Dick. Give him my love, Frieda, & tell him I'm *very* sorry we can't meet, tell him I'm 'digalon' about it. I told him you loved him. Aren't I a good messenger?

Well, Frieda, you *will* be in Bombay on the 21st? I hope my train is to time, so I can meet you at Victoria. Oh Glory be to all the angels.

Que je t'aime

Au voir

Alun

FA note: Between Sept 5th
('Sunday morning')
and Sept 12th

214565 Lt. A. Lewis
GHQ Intelligence School
KARACHI

Frieda, don't read me until Dick's gone & you're by yourself. Put me away for now - - - - now. It's late tonight and the evening went through my fingers. I spent two hours talking on Michael's bed till 8. Then I came back & lay in a bath of cool water till the dusk had fallen. I was playing with the gentle images & the dark melancholy images of dusk & then I said 'Why should I? I must refuse these gentle and natural images & the seductions of the dark & exclude them from anything I write'. I shook the water & the night away & went across to the school to do a certain amount of work. But the man who sits next to me in class buttonholed me, he was sweating & a bit drunk & very excited & it turned out that a pal of his had thrown a glass of brandy over the Anglo Indian hotel manager where they were dining because the oriental gentleman had refused a drink & Italy had 'fallen'. All of which pretty overture concluded with the military police leading this patriotic young subaltern to the cooler & it completely spoiled my friend's dinner, you see, and he feels rotten about the whole show because apparently if Italy hadn't fallen this would never have happened. Isn't it sad that Italy had to fall, Frieda, & all these lamentable repercussions in the Far East? Oh darling, what bloody idiots there certainly are. And this took all night, listening to this & smoothing him down, so I haven't done my work or read a beautiful poem or had a worthy thought, but simply bought this gallant young English captain a couple of gins & let him repeat his story to me ad nauseam, & tried to tell him to let the other silly bastard take what's due to him. Shabby dusty answer.

Are you pleased with being in Poona, darling? Is Dick big and placid and thoughtful and ham-handed? Are you staying in the coffin rooms of the Poona Hotel or the Napier or the nice little one by the station with the blue lights outside it? Did you enjoy the journey, & the grey rocks & caves you pass the evening before you arrived? That's where I saw the tall red anthills & I was thinking of you & so it became the end of the poem. It's quite near Bombay, Poona is, does it feel near? Do you want it to be near? I haven't heard from you since you left Madras. Did the mali have a new watering can? Did the Beveridge talk go over well? I'm sure it did but it's proper to ask. I'm full of questions tonight – I just want to talk & talk. It won't be long now & we can talk then with nothing in the world to come between, our voices will mingle in the air & hardly need to go past our lips to reach each other. Are you glad? I'm glad, Frieda, I'm so glad we're going to meet. We *are* going to meet, aren't we? I wish I heard from you. Tomorrow, I say every day. I will hear tomorrow.

I would like you to meet Michael. He's oh very very nice. Quiet and witty and good dark eyes & loose black hair fine & straight & a good pianist & full of a boyish hatred & loathing for the world he sees out here, and a destructive mind because the cleanness in him wishes healthily to destroy the filth that is nourished here. And his ears are in a bad way – some fungoid affection that is filling the bone & cavities right up to the nose with pus & water. I know I'll leave him in hospital a week tomorrow & I suppose like all my friends I won't see him again. And like myself I don't mind. I do mind, it hurts badly, every time with a little addition of bitterness, but I grow stronger each time, & prouder, & remember that one more little part of the world has some sentient portion of it that occasionally thinks good of me, or holds a little warmth for me. Which is all one has any right to ask or need.

Frieda, I've had very exciting news from Gweno today. She sent 'The Orange Grove' to Connolly at *Horizon*; I've told you how he's refused to print anything of mine since I had *Raiders' Dawn* approved by the G.B.P.; and although I don't like his polity of bumlicking America & printing obituaries and essays on Oscar Wilde & all the dead & gones, I was narked by his stolid refusal to accept anything. And 'The Orange Grove' crashed in like that! Gweno received the proofs by return of post!! Hooray! I am full of vindictive delight. The hospital story she sent to John Lehmann & he accepted it for *New Writing* 'with thanks' – & also two poems. I don't think this feeling of gratification is illegitimate. I am really glad – I could say happy – about it, and I feel glad enough to think a long way ahead & envisage the bigger work that I rarely let myself consider. But 'The Orange Grove' was flesh of my flesh & they've approved of it. I'm ridiculously glad.

Gweno gave me much sound advice, also. I'll show you these letters she's just sent me. One upbraiding me for the sensualism of my images, one quietly telling me I will discover my impartial self out here & will become isolated and write infinitely better because of it: and she'll no longer find any Gweno & any Alun in it then and she'll be even lonelier, but she wants me to make this evolution because my writing needs it. When she decides to speak she has a powerful authority over me, seeming to speak inside me. Mostly she doesn't say a word, but lets the wind blow.

Give my love to Dick if I don't have time to squeeze a letter in for him, too. Curse this perpetual not-meeting; there are so many things one can't do anything about. Famines one can prevent – why don't they? Oh Christ why don't they? But meeting Dick seems impossible: but it doesn't matter because Dick & I are old friends & we know how things are. Give him a hug for me.

Goodnight, Frieda darling. I'll write to you again & once again before we meet. Oh *please* let us meet. Please, please.

xxxx   your   xxxx   lover   xx   Alun

214565 *Lieut. A. Lewis*
6th Bn. S.W.B.
Intschool
KARACHI

Sept. 12th Monday

Frieda darling,

It's very late tonight and the chaprasi wants to lock the building & put the lights out & Alun wants to sleep because he's got a test of aircraft recognition tomorrow morning & will be out on an exercise all tomorrow night. And Frieda'll be climbing into her berth now too, somewhere between Mettupalayam & Arkonam and time is moving towards one time & places are moving towards one place, and all I want to say, dearest, is that I won't have any peace until I have the reality & assurance of your earthly body with me, and that I'll meet you God willing when your train arrives in Bombay on Tuesday the 21st. Godspeed.

I've been thinking & feeling a lot today – not more than any other day, but it seems to be resolving itself today into a clearer understanding of life. So that I know that it is not a matter of enchantment but of living & dying, being with & being without, losing and finding, trying & failing, sharing & not sharing. Oh God, it's the real texture of my life, and it will have all my weaknesses & all the ways in which I am disappointing & disconcerting in it. And it will have you as you are & were & will be. And I want to talk to you about all the sadness & all the joy & all the hardness & all the gentleness we've begun. I want to be with you where nobody else is, just for long enough for us to understand what it is. You *will* be there, Frieda, won't you? Otherwise perhaps we will never understand, never attain. It's the hardest thing I have ever tried, Frieda, it is. I love you & want to be with you, that we should know each other more.

I won't write anything else now, darling. I'm leaving here on Sat the 18th at 7 a.m., arriving in Bombay at 10.30 am on Tuesday. I'll take my kit to the Taj if I've time. If I'm late & your train has come in when I get to V.T. station I'll go on to the Taj & meet you there if you're not in the station refreshment room having lunch. I'll look in there first.

Auf wiedersehn, gipsy mealie-frock

Ever, ever, Alun

Frieda, Frieda,

I'm sad to think of you sleeping in that rocking train tonight again, Frieda darling. Sad, sad, sad, oh *sad*. But in the morning you'll wake up in the Blue Mountains & at 11 you'll be hugging Gilly and in the afternoon when I'm plodding out into the *bloody* hot mountains for a three day exercise you'll be laying your cool beautiful body down between the sheets and sinking through thought & feeling into a true sleep. The sleep you and the baby need and are enriched by. But you'll be so tired, I know, you'll be aching & dull with tiredness and the dreadful emptiness of fatigue. And I'll be lying in the dry valleys in my clothes and sweating mosquito cream & I know I'll be so restless for you & so angry and aching at the absence of you. I shall be hard pressed to stick the sun and the marching or running Thursday & Friday & Saturday. I'm not as strong as I need to be, it sometimes so exhausts me that it's agony, just pure physical agony & horror to endure. And I'm not at all fit now, after Karachi's languid talking shop. And you know that like Caliban I have been translated ('monster, thou art translated') and I so loved and loved a beautiful beautiful girl called Frieda Buttery that I think I have strained myself just a wee bit because I had been virginal and continent for a long long time and something in me was surprised and exhausted by that much greater wave that over-flowed in me; and it was always not enough, not enough, and this other little virgin thing murmuring 'But you two lovers need months, years, time, time, not to be exhausted but to attain a calmer fruition.' And I don't know whether the little sigh & murmur is right, and all I know is that it was a vain and impossible murmur that we must, we simply had to overwhelm. So this evening there

Wed Sept 43

20a   Midnight   214565 Lt A Lewis,
                               6th Bn, South Wales Borderers
                               ABPO 21.

Frieda, Frieda,   TUESDEE

I'm sad to think of you sleeping in
that rocking train tonight again, Frieda darling.
Sad, sad, sad, oh _sad_. But in the morning
you'll wake up in the Blue Mountains.
At 11 you'll be hugging Gilly and in the
afternoon when I'm plodding out into the
bloody hot mountains for a three day
exercise you'll be laying your cool beautiful
body down between the sheets and sinking
through thought & feeling into a true sleep.
The sleep you and the baby need and are
enriched by. But you'll be so tired, I know;
you'll be aching & dull with tiredness and
the dreadful emptiness of fatigue. And I'll
be lying in the dry valleys in my clothes &
sweating mosquito cream & I know I'll be
so restless for you & so angry and aching
at the absence of you. I shall be hard
pressed to stick the sun and the marching
& running on Thursday & Friday & Saturday.
I'm not as strong as I need to be, it
sometimes so exhausts me that it's agony,
just pure physical agony & horror to endure.
And I'm not at all fit now, after
Karachi's languid talking shop. And you
know that like Caliban "I have been
translated ('monster, thou art translated.')
and I so loved and loved a beautiful
beautiful girl called Frieda Buttery that
I think I have strained myself just a wee

138

was a soccer match and I asked if I could play in the team to overwhelm this little voice in a physical effort. And my lungs were bursting and I was hot & dry & wet wet wet all over, and I kept on until I felt better and I ran & leaped & kicked the silly friendly ball & banged my dear Welsh soldier mates. And darling all the time all the time my body was feeling you & feeling itself in you and you holding it in you and the longing of being on a football field and not in you. And that is very strange for games usually enchant & absorb me & I don't feel anything but as Mrs. Battle did about whist 'the rigour of the game'. And I've been hungry all night to come at last to you & write to you. But it's been so long & it's so late now & I need a long deep dewy sleep & I'm only going to have a short one & it can't be helped, for there is this to you which says Must Must Must. I'll be so glad when you get to Highfield, Frieda, & I can come to you there so easily because I was there & it *is* me & it is you without any doubt or any complexity or difficulty or strain, because there was nothing to prevent us there when I did come first nor all the time I was there with you & Gillykins & me.

And this ache for you hasn't begun yet. It's only stirred in its sleep.

Your letter was here for me. It moved me very much. It was the only letter I read of the pile here for me. I couldn't read the others. Nor can I talk about your letter. You were jealous of Sister Cranfield holding my hand when I was under the anaesthetic & I'm reminding you of that before you hasten to chide me for saying this – that I'm jealous of Preeks Purves for kissing you & Arthur Hope for loving you & Paul's father for loving you but not him so much, *and you* for telling me they love you. And the people I should be jealous of for loving you I'm not jealous of, and I'm not saying I'm right, in fact you can *easily* prove I'm ridiculous & wrong, but I'm just telling you that I am. And if you say I'm not to be I still am & if you say they—— oh put your arms round me in the window in the night breeze in quiet in nakedness. There, what silliness was I saying?

Do you want to know how I got back? Read it quickly it's not interesting. I didn't find a truck there & I was feeling dull and hard & nothing, nothing, except a little dry dull bewilderment, & I telephoned & asked them to send a truck. And then a little Punjabi woman gave me some postcards with a man's name on it. She had a child & she had come to Poona to look for this man & she couldn't find him & did I know Ram Charand & I didn't & she wouldn't go to the G.P.O. or the police & she sat down on the platform where the trains come in & I asked her if she had any money & she said no with her head & I offered her a rupee & she bowed her head & said no with the back of her bowed head & I left her & went in a taxi to send your wire to Krishnan.*

There was a beggar woman there slapping her shrivelled guts & I only gave her two annas & felt ashamed & gave her no more, and than I sat in the Poona Chinese restaurant & suddenly the sky became beautiful with sunset & a leafy tree moved its branches as gently as your hand moved in its sleep. And I felt very very very quiet. And then the lorry came & we drove back & then there was Harry Tudor with a badly hidden smile on his face & I knew he was genuinely glad & happy that I'd come back & he fussed about, emptying my box till I kicked him off to bed & I went over to the mess to reintroduce myself.

And today after the soccer match I felt I had to tell somebody I love you & say your name & Jack Gush walked back with me from the field & instead of saying all that I just suddenly put my arm round his shoulder & hugged him with my dripping sweaty head & he didn't guess & said 'Funny old bugger'. Darling I won't be able to write till Sunday. Say it doesn't matter.

Say we love each other. Come? XXXX
XXXXX Alun

Wednesday morning:

As you're going up the hill and are nearly nearly home I'm coming through the bazaar to meet your train & I've missed you so much & it's been such a long time since Monday, darling, and I can't stay long. I must rush off at 1.30 to put my equipment on and get away on this god damned exercise. I slept profoundly last night & woke with a deep reluctance to stir the sleeping voice, but it had to get up & do all those furious things. I wonder when your letter will reach me – not this week. But it doesn't matter. It doesn't matter. It does it doesn't. I was having a shower bath after the soccer match last night and a boy was singing with the sweet tone of an English thrush

> Wheree'er you walk
> Cool gales shall fan the glade

I couldn't see him. I could see the sky blazing with an unexpected sunset that drove out of the black clouds & threw a wild & tranquil rainbow over the valley. It was very lovely under the cold water watching & listening.

I can't *say* anything, Frieda, it's no use saying anything. I must join in the rush & you are more securely & certainly within me in silence.

I wonder where & when we will be next. And I'm sorry you felt sick yesterday morning & this morning & I'm glad you're home.

I can't say anything about Bombay. I keep on seeing the little flower boy smiling at the door of our room.

> Goodbye darling
> All my love & longing
> Alun

*Freda's note: Wallace's assistant, to send a car to meet me.

Frieda dearest,

About a mile & a half away there is a beautiful lake. I want to sit by it to write to you, instead of in this cooped up tent with an oldish rough officer writing to his young dumb wife on whom he dotes & dotes. I must go out of here, but my feet are all blistered and the sun is harsh. I'll wait till evening, then go to the lake with you.

Darling Frieda, It's been such a rush since I got here on Monday night. I haven't unpacked or sat & thought or felt myself to be at all. Except wildly & transiently all the time the sensations & images & echoes and recurrences of you in my blood & in my mind have accompanied me all the time. Yesterday we marched all day over some hills & at evening debouched into a valley through which we threaded our way in darkness till after midnight. Then a couple of hours of plans & conferences with Alfie Aslett, & then a voyage by water & a landing at 6.30 a.m. & a dawn attack up a range of hills. After that was over we marched back to camp & here I am. There were times last night, when we marched after dark & during the early hours of this morning, when I felt an unbearable fatigue. Literally unbearable. I told the Colonel I *had* to sleep & he let me lie down on the grass for 5 minutes & sleep & then he woke me. During the awful vacant intervals of fatigue my mind was like a large empty reception chamber in which you & I sat with great spaces about us and a sense of trouble: not trouble but of indeterminateness, of having to wait a long time yet before the power of knowing & acting comes on us. At other times, even when I was fully exercised in the messages & problems & exertions of the exercise you came beautifully and irresistibly into me and I joined you gladly and secretly & was proud. When I had to stand once & wait for about 30 minutes in the darkness at the corner of a paddy field I was so tormented in my hollow tired mind by the realisation of your absence that I prayed that I should stop thinking. Today, marching back to camp I have been feeling a sense of loss, & anger against the smooth counsel of resignation and a fierce unwillingness to be satisfied with this life of camp & physical labour and war training. I still feel this loss & it aches & I am a bit flat and sad.

There is also something imprisoned. It was imprisoned by us, perhaps the morning that we packed our suitcases. It was locked away when you left me at Poona & I hated it being locked away then. I wanted it terribly much on Poona station those last few minutes but perhaps it was wiser than us. I'm sure it is wiser than me. And I am nothing without it. I am waiting for it to speak. Perhaps I'm wrong in thinking it's imprisoned in you; perhaps you're free. Though you are so uncannily close to me in the moods & *times* of feeling that I feel you are so, too.

A week ago today we were looking from our window, late on Friday afternoon, and deciding to go up to Malabar gardens & see the evening come to the little people. Later we had a gimlet so clad in ice that it was like chipping a water hole in an ice floe to reach the licker. Then there was a cabaret in which a man shook a tin uncouthly & coins fell about him & the audience liked the falling of money better than the falling of manna which they wouldn't have understood: but manna was falling in the room, on you, on me. Later still we slept. I can remember these things behind a gauze. They also are imprisoned & insulated and with me it is always so when it has been profound & far-reaching. For a long time I am like a chrysalid: then at last the certainty emerges & I glow & am blessed & perhaps write a poem. You wonder in your letter whether I will. Can I fail to? I feel so dwarfed & stilled & humbled by what happened to us. I know it was something more than either of us, that it is a directive force which will achieve itself in us whether we oppose it or not, whether it brings pain or not. And I am content perforce to wait. Some things one dare not force. You spoke very bravely & forwardly in your letter: about the heart, the blood ('oh easily in the blood' you said; & it is true) & the acknowledging over which there is a veil. How or when this will come to pass, we don't know. But it is always coming to pass, always moving towards it. I haven't slept for two nights on this exercise & I've sweated & exerted myself hugely, & yet I'm not tired because of this sleepless longing for the veil to fall off, the reality to come. It grieves & worries me, too; Frieda, beloved, the untamed wildness is away in the jungle about its own ways & we must let it be so. It's the only really fundamental truth we mean. It's the only miracle over which we have no control. And if we could control it it would no longer be a miracle. Let it bide, beloved.

And to you your child growing in you & to me this barren and unsatisfying soldiering. I am in love with your child. Sometimes it will seem as though you are bearing me. For of course you are. Such is the nearness in us.

Love Alun

214565 *Lt. A. Lewis*
6th Bn. South Wales Borderers
ABPO. 21

[Received by FA October 11th]

Frieda darling,

I don't know whether I can write to you or not, I seem to be stunned. I don't know why. Perhaps you're stunned, too. I haven't heard from you yet at all and I don't know how it could be right except we were alone & far away somewhere. I don't know how I can write this letter or the poem except we were together a long way from anywhere. I don't know what has become of the armour, the tenderness, the afterglow that was always in us. I've been trying to find my way to it. I swam in the lake this evening, looking for it in the easy motions of my limbs in the unembarrassed water, and in the sky & the distance. I borrowed Beethoven's 8th & *Eine kleine Nachtmusik* and listened with my nerves & all my mind to the significant branchings, energies and murmurs of the music and I was so nearly attaining it that I felt pain for the first time. Now I'm hopelessly shut into the camp life again. A soccer match, a disjointed conversation at dinner, a visit to the reading room to see how things go: oh and a longing beyond words & beyond feeling. It makes me feel grey and futile, being unable like this. To have your hand on my head, to feel the goodness beginning in your touch. I feel such a dolt, Frieda, and whatever it was that happened, now seems to have been so swift & so beyond me & greater than me that I sit like a lump in my chair. I've been reading that dreadful Kafka novel *America*, and it's shoved me into the slime of untouchable things, as when things have a bad feel like some kinds of felt and you can't really feel them at all. Frieda, I want you *now*, so much, oh Christ so much. If it had happened slower, so that I needn't have closed up like this & excluded my bewildered self like this. Did it happen too quickly for *you*? I know it did. And it now seems incomprehensible that we were in a window, high & unassailable and perfected & you spoke of goddess & god; and I knew only the charm and not the hardness that succeeds it. Yet I *did* know of the hardness because it is always my ancient enemy, and has an old claim on me. But you'd so spirited it away that I couldn't – I get no nearer by talking, Frieda darling; it's the old childish hankering that I haven't outgrown, the hankering for a continuous happiness. Happiness brings its own nemesis; feeling its own atrophy. Doesn't it? Why do we dread it so, then? A week has gone & I have been nothing. I was thinking it would be a week of intensity, but it hasn't ; and I feel only the queerness of it taking things into its own hands & disposing me not as I wish but as it chooses. Maybe it's inevitable: I think we have done something much more than we can understand & it won't resolve itself in a week or a year. It's only sad because when we are together our bodies & beings have their own natural and simple peace, and a mutual ecstasy contains us without us willing or helping it. Separately, the implications begin to muster & burn and defame & fight. I must get used to them, I suppose. I am their house. But how I ache back for that utter angelic beauty that we ignited in space in being *together*. Darling, I'm so dull now, & I sleep so deeply & wake without a thought in my head, no point of recognition, nothing within me to start & give direction to the day. And it could be so otherwise, I know. I can't bear the man who has just come in & owns the other half of this hut & is spraying it with a flit-gun & smoking a heavy pipe. If he talks I shake with a nervous 'tic'. When you were going to sleep, swiftly & steeply in my arms, your hands would twitch sometimes and it filled me with tenderness for you and I loved you very deeply & gently when your hand jumped involuntarily in mine, and all I want now is to feel that happen again and to soothe and bless it away. When it was like that it was as if we had come to each other out of some brittle nowhere

where nothing mattered. And perhaps it isn't true, I don't know, but it couldn't be better on this earth & in this life than to feel as if we had come from an old negative world into the simple & supreme syllable of love. It's only now when I think of Frieda Aykroyd in Coonoor, & Alun Lewis in the South Wales Borderers going their disparate & necessary ways that I grieve for the poverty and naked-ness of spirit in which we became minute and splendid as a grain of sand and were capable of surpassing whatever had & does now prevent us. Frieda darling, I'm sorry to be trying all the time to reach it: I might do better to be writing lightly of simpler things, of how the hours have actually passed here, of falling in the mud in my clean suit last night going down to the camp cinema to see *The Reluctant Dragon* – have you seen it? It's quite delightful in parts, lovely colours and a beautiful singing train rolling along the line as happy as the day is long as long as things are going well: & Goofy trying to ride a hunter & failing to win the recalcitrant horse's respect & confidence, and baby Weems who spoke beautiful American the day he was born and had a lovely conversation with Einstein & Shaw & then suddenly lapsed back into baby gurglings shortly after splitting the atom & was forgotten by an avid & offended public. It's a nice film except for the flat insipid drawings of people and scenery, that pretty-pretty hallmark of the Disney school of plebeian art. I read a nice little essay by Max Beerbohm too which I am sending on to you. It's very gentil and proud, an old man attacking an age of low standards, & doing it with impeccable dignity & lightness of touch.

I haven't done anything else at all except slip down to the lake on Saturday evening and lie in the water watching the sun-set up the wild hill sides & the steep rocky gulfs grow slowly ethereal and untrue. I'm going into Poona tomorrow to a conference & I want to buy a battery for my torch & books for the unit library and socks and Elastoplast and some Xmas presents for home. And I want to return in the afternoon to find your letter at last, and even if you are feeling awful you will find some part of yourself that can just write a little note to me in your handwriting. And if you are feeling alright will you copy out 'The Map' & 'Hands' and 'Being of Soldiers' & 'The Peasants' for me so that I can read them and find my way to those other poems that are so stifled & unwritten in me all the time?

It appears now as if I won't want you to send *For Whom the Bell Tolls* to me for a long time to come. It's depressing to see no definite term to this long long preparation we've been enduring – I've had more than is healthy of pretending enemies & it becomes like a nauseating outgrown schoolboy's game, & I do it with distaste. But perhaps you are glad & perhaps you are right. I only want what I feel is necessary to me. I know I'll be released by it, although I'm not a bloodthirster. I can't accept anything here, not even the beautiful lake.

I will write to Gilly only when I am untrammelled. Perhaps in a day or two, perhaps much longer. Next week I'll be away for six days & won't be able to write to you. Will you please make my silence into letters & thought? I'm worried. How slowly and difficultly we *become*.

I won't write any more tonight, Frieda darling. I'll let this deep sleep have its way. I'll be alright soon, I expect. I should be used to my unsuccessful self by now. It's good for me too, humbling me so completely. I don't show it to anyone: I've learnt that much savoir faire. I show it to you because you will understand it and be willing to take it, as you did the last day I was in Coonoor, in the narrow ride in the wood among the dead leaves. One way or another I make a lot of shadows where I go. Everywhere I go, inevitably. Somehow I become downcast. I want you to know of this poverty, for you say often I am rich as Croesus & endowed with divine bounties at birth & it's only half true for I'm as poor as bloody old

Lazarus also and it's in poverty that you must find me if you love me.

Goodnight, Frieda darling
My mark   X
Ever love & love & Poverty
Alun

214565 Lt. A. Lewis
6th Bn. South Wales Borderers
ABPO 21

Oct. 8th.

Frieda darling

At last your letter. Nine days it took: the first word at all I've had from you since the train took you away from me, and then for ages nothing & nothing as if you were Mrs. Owen. The jokes in worst taste that the world plays on us are those in which inefficient postal services compel brainstorms and nervous prostrations in those who wait, & imagine horrible inarticulations in the beloved because there is no word, nothing. Oh damn the post for getting me into such agonies. Each day this week has been a bitter & as it were vital rebuff & distress – I looked & there was nothing. And today is the last day for a fortnight that I shall get any letters for I'm moving off in the darkness in a few hours on a stuffy and endless exercise from which I won't return for *so* long. I was fearful that I wouldn't have your letter to take with me. But when I came down to the Mess after the cloudburst at dusk tonight, considerably fatigued by the day's flap and bustle, there miraculously was your letter, and I am sure Gilly's delight in your return couldn't have been simpler or more natural than mine. I felt just like a child and your letter caressed me as I read it and my apprehension became its naïve and trusting opposite, delight and self-surrender. Bless you for your letter.

It is a dear dear letter too. I'm sorry I caused you so much pre-occupation with one theme, darling: and that I should have mentioned it in my second letter to you makes me cross. It *is* uncanny how we seem to think the same things, quite independently. I don't think them because you are thinking them. It isn't telepathic. It's because we are in the same place in eternity: our alonenesses are identical, our spirits have the same calluses, and the same ferocities, and the same vulnerable sides. I rarely feel that I am thinking the same things as you, though sometimes I do. But generally I think in the heart of a wide and stony aloneness and I simply observe that you also thought just that just then. And I don't understand why it should be like that, unless it be by the allegory of the two beasts we whispered about at the window and on the bed, the yellow-eyed proud soft moving beasts that go their own way and in some clearing in the jungle sometimes come upon each other and become thereby sublime. But I swore not to mention their existence, nor will I again.

You *were* able to write to me, and I have not been able to write to you, and that is bitter to me, but I can take it like that if it must be. I have an 'old' feeling that is queer to me and makes me try to laugh it away – in vain. I'll tell you what it sees and says, it's a strange maturity in me that *does* exist in me, I know; and in many many people I've met it, in young peasant children & collier children, girls of ten with lots of younger brothers & sisters to mother in poverty, and boys who've had this war in all its devilry like Michael. And it always accompanies a youngness that also has its way.

It says that I am older than you. It says that you have lived in a part of you only, and the you I encountered in July, whom I loved all the week and lay by the lake with in Toda-land and met again in Bombay among trains and lotuses, little hotels and the sea, you aren't anyone but you, but Frieda, whom I know by your eyes and hair and nose and hips and legs, little colt. And that I am older than Frieda is, because some things seem to attack you for the first time and I realise seriously and a little sadly that they have happened to me already, for good & all, & I am past them for ever. I knew you were upset when I told the man we were going and when you said 'It seems such a wrong & so wasteful that we must go different ways'; I heard my oldness saying clearly to you 'No, it isn't a pity,

Frieda'. And then he shut up, because I'm very conscious that this oldness is precocious in me and isn't supposed to go on parade. But I *have* experienced that dreadful inevitability long ago, darling. A year ago it came to flower in me, a dark flower like D.H. Lawrence's blue gentians, and I bled and bled inside me and then I healed myself lying awake in the troopship listening to the ceaseless throb of the engines and accepting the hurt to my being that the remorseless engines inflicted with their indifferent and steadfast purpose. *And I know I had gone!* That's a tremendous truth, darling, to know one has gone. I wrote myself off then and I shall never go back to before that again. And when it happened again, sweet, it happened in the morning darkness when I was unprepared & without defence, and it turned gentle in me, gentle and dreadfully, wonderfully heartbreaking, and I was lucky to be in your arms in the darkness because with you I can do impossible things, I can cry. So when it came to the arrangements of going I was very mature and there was no desperation in my simple wish to leave fresh flowers where we'd been so happy, but just a sense of rightness and order. And I make my own order where I can, for there's none in the world. The storms that broke on us tonight have soaked my bed, my little table, my books, overturned my hurricane lamp and split kerosene on the darling little Cambridge Univ. Press essay of Max Beerbohm's that I was going to send you. And in a couple of hours I must get up and dress & go off in a lorry and embark in a ship at dawn and spend days among mangrove creeks & mountains. And all the time in that disorder I try to keep inviolate my own inmost and by no means steady order. And I would like you to think of me that way, darling, as in some spiritual fastness desiring a little tidiness of the soul, a serenity that can advise and influence the turbulence that I share, the violence and mischances that become my own emotions, yet cannot overwhelm the tidiness that you help me to make somewhere, I don't know where, in the world I am.

Well, he's said you're young, & there we go again, there's your oldness smiling wryly over your shoulder as you read this, saying 'Ah, but I also am old & he is young'. Panther!! The clearing again in the jungle. Go away from my waterhole. I am drinking. Drink with me. Go away. Stay. Go away that you may always stay. What else does he say?

In seeking this soul tidiness he becomes shrewd, not successfully, but he tries. He tries to assess & balance, and when some frightened & defenceless voice starts making slanderous allegations he chides them like Arthur Happell in a disorderly court & teaches them respect. And he says in his shrewd pipesmoking voice 'It will be anything but easy or painless'. I haven't got much patience with him when he's shrewd, but there it is, he's got his feet on the earth, he's got his allotment and his insurance policy and you can't get away from him easily because he's so fair-minded. In a way he's very manly and he's willing for hurt, he's not insensitive. But oh Frieda how near your are and other times how far, and how you are always beginning in me & every consummation is only a lucid and transcendent statement of the beginning, of things not even yet beginning to begin in us. And what can he say to that, or to Beethoven who is also saying just that. Beethoven is always saying that, and his wretchedness and agony are when he realises that there is no time left for the beginnings to become. Some people realise it casually and shrug their shoulders. With Beethoven it wracked his body as well as his mind. But of course he could do nothing except state it, and its affirmation is always the purest beauty one can apprehend, whether it is music for violin viola & violin-cello or just the soul realising it & affirming it utterly & silently in the night in love.

I'm better darling, you can see that, can't you: the sickness [in] my last letter is finished & I'm better & you've made me better. But I'm still protected from the youngness that married us and can grieve so terribly, like Gilly losing her white heather. Tonight I really am tired, because I've worked bloody hard all day, and I just want to lie in your arms, Frieda, and sleep. But I wouldn't want to leave you in the dark & I'd have to soon. I loathe that. So perhaps my oldness is wisest in his strange old desire to be alone while the war and the preparations for war go on & on & on. Did you mind me crying, Frieda? It was very gentle of you to take my weeping like that, my inner confidence that would be so easy to misunderstand.

And again I've written nothing of the happening things & the byplay. Nor have I gone nearer than I dare to us. Is it an unsatisfactory letter? Please take it as it is, darling.

I've had a lot of letters this week. Only one touched me at all till yours today. That was from Michael, who is also one of our kin, and is shy about himself & makes me a little shy too. I'd like you to meet him.

Frieda beloved, give Gilly my love too. I'll write all I can darling. Please wait.

Always. All
Alun

19th P.S. And in fact you were
in bed & writing to me, for I've
just had your letter of the 14th
on getting back to the camp at
midnight.

Frieda,

10 p.m. You may be abed, may be reading, maybe not, maybe the hostess with the strange & fascinating confidence and élan that sets you a little apart by the same quality as it brings you dangerously near. I'm in a queer place now, and I shall be in a similar place the night before I have my first taste of the Japanese. It's one of those macabre and faintly mocking rehearsals of dire events that only take place in war, and one doesn't take them seriously. The imagination projects itself carefully, & withdraws from the rough prevision of reality like a snail whose horn has touched a hairy leaf. Tomorrow I shall be in the thick of a mock battle; tonight, leaning over the darkness, I thought neatly & precisely of the odds for and against the survival of my military body; and they are mainly governed by the intelligence of my colonel. He has a weak hankering to *see* things. Unless his eyes see, his mind cannot grasp. So he must be up in the front, & see the puff where the machine gun is located. If companies have to attack he always chooses the approach which allows him to *see* them, rather than a covered approach giving them concealment. I decided I had better bend my brains, and the influence which I have over him, to guide him to safer counsels. This is heretical talk, but it's quite true and is my main motive in staying where I am rather than taking the seductive captaincy they dangled at me in Karachi, which, as George Oldridge pointed out, would be much better place for me to preserve my military brain for further employment!! It's all rather like the

gambits of suburban parties & intrigues, this thoughtful choosing and positioning of oneself. I think I'm right and am prepared to forsake the security of tenure that so many people so rightmindedly prefer.

This wasn't the letter I started to write. I might say this in a letter to Michael or Dick. Are you satisfied that I should say it to you? I think you are: although I spent far more time in the darkness just now singing 'Una Furtiva Lacrima' and floating among questions and images of enchantment. Frieda, you have excited more questions in my little cosmos that I can deal with. Hence the great difficulties that seem to hold me in thought & feeling nowadays. Even in the unnatural lucidity of late July, when I never needed any food and wrote my last poems, I knew that these unmanageable colonies were forming in myself, and I said by Mallmund lake that love would not be easy and joyous or a continuous sharing of happiness for either of us. I don't know even whether it will have that long physical reality of nearness & sharing time & touch that love asks for. Do you know? You know more than me. There are some forms of love that I am incapable just now of understanding and it would be wrong of me to speak of love without that greater understanding, for I would hurt you perhaps. I read Richard Hillary's *Last Enemy* yesterday & failed to understand. Yet when I read you Koestler's essay on Hillary it was all too painfully clear to me. In the same way when I listened with you to Alun Lewis reading his poems it was unbearably clear to me & it was a necessity that the needle should stick on the monkeys loping obscenely the monkeys loping obscenely the monkeys loping obscenely the monkeys loping obscenely – & click, the door of the safe snapped to & I haven't felt that poignant anguish & all its warmth since. This severe and limited sentience is I think defensive. Damn this rolling & creaking, la mer s'enrage, le bateau ivre roule, je ne suis pas marin.

156

The problem is so utterly simple, darling, and so utterly insoluble. I would come to you through all evil elements and death-surges; and yet I cannot come to you except when I am with you. (This isn't true.) When I am with you the problem has ceased to exist. *We are.* That is complete. At all other times this love is a cruelty to the other love I receive and have given, which so powerfully shaped and directed me that its compulsions & recollection are as normal & real as my daily answers to the daily tasks & situations in which I live in the army. You know all this; as you know that those words & feelings are said & felt for ever and compel & alter for ever & one is never the same afterwards as before. And I would not have imagined that this also could happen which happened to us, nor that we could enter in of ourselves into such liberty and such untrammelled ways. It was bound to be restricted in many ways. The most obvious is the impediment of time. We have seen each other little, & there will always be long periods of not seeing. And the other obstructions lie inside us and sometimes they choke me. I've fought very hard you know, darling, since I met you, very very hard. Really fought and fought. And when it's been very hard I've made myself endure the hardness & not try to end it in some false way. And I know we need a long time for ourselves to be understood. And yet always there is this other unfettered heaven we can enter into more easily than anyone in the world & inhabit without hardness or failing. You knew, more than I, much much more you knew you could make me love in a way I thought impossible to me; and I know now that you have much more love to waken in my body than has yet stirred. And in me there has never been such ease as you made. Ease on earth is nothing. But ease in those unapproachable heavens is scarcely to be spoken of afterwards. You wouldn't want me to love you for that, but I do & always will. I shall always say somewhere, deeply & secretly, 'It was she'. I go about the earth with greater freedom & more strength of judgment from that sweet knowledge. And can come to you more easily because of it. And am not afraid of you or of me. There is only one fear in me at all. That is *for* Gweno. I love her and can hurt her too much, I would prefer to lie or die or not be born than hurt her like that. Oh Frieda darling, I don't know what all this going to become. Do you, beloved? I am not whining. I'm quite clear to myself, and human. I want you to talk to me in this quietness, this lateness of the night, this love that gathers us into itself and liberates the beauty in us and moves us to a wonderful musical apprehension that has its exquisite way with us, in the night, in our bodies, in our soul. Now there is nothing to do but to sleep, and I go to sleep very easily and quietly, to rest for tomorrow. Tomorrow is like the Monday we left Bombay, or the Tuesday I left Coonoor: *tomorrow*.

Goodnight, Frieda, I'm in your sleeping arms. (My story was on the radio tonight & I didn't listen to it.)

The day after tomorrow: yesterday was an active day; sweat, blisters, maps, iron biscuits & dates, and a long cool sleep among the sand dunes all the milky night. I contrived to swim at dusk when the sea was the dull red of distant conflagrations. Now I'm changed and in (fairly) clean clothes and it's all over except the return to camp. Tomorrow I shall see the window at which we sat: I shall be the horizon we contemplated. Last night, lying in the dunes I thought how we let the breeze make love between us in the luminous freedom of the last darkness before dawn, and how by moving closer and locking our arms a little closer we excluded the breeze and were front to front and cool and simple together. Many things I've been unable to remember came to me last night lying alone and caught my throat with that sharp pang we feel for some delight that cannot be recaptured. Sitting in Malabar gardens, going by taxi to eat & dance at the Taj Mahal, you sitting like a babu at a desk in the bowels of the G.P.O., you standing in the quartier latin corridor of the Hotel Marina on Sunday afternoon after the cinema saying 'Alright, pay the taxi. Let's stay', and being somehow unwilling to look at me till we were together. Has your sunburn gone? My shoulders are still pimply. I wear overalls dyed green for jungle camouflage & my body is a dirty green after an exercise & when I bath the water runs away green off me. But my body is very well & happy and sends its love to you. He sends his love to her also very much.

Are we going to write this play of ours, Frieda? I don't know enough to do it. I can *see* it, & feel it, and I intend to make some prose studies for it next week if I get any peace. I can best do it in prose – a series of chapters or 'moments' of thought, cast as a reverie or an incident. But the hard & essential conversation I can't manage. We could do it together, by speaking it. I imagine the long rhythm will begin with the invasion of Malaya; the fall of Singapore & the departure of the military males from all their clubs & then Burma & news of deaths & hospitals. Then the threat of invasion (I don't know at all how they took that) – and then the long anti-climax when invasion didn't come. And it's in this long anti-climax that I think the greatest excitement lies. For the further the 'enemy' retreats the farther & more hopelessly distantly is he followed, so the victory as it grows swallows & extinguishes the victors until there is a threat of extinction in the final envisaged victory, as there must be for people without a purpose behind their fighting. And there must be the individual disasters which seem cruel and yet unimportant & irrelevant to the main motive & tide of events. And the Indians – I don't know how to write of them – do you know what they would say & do? Their inability to be anything positive or to experience either defeat or danger or risk of loss; their awful social complexes, their profiteering slickness and their pauper passive suffering? I can see it best from my own point of view, that is as a man with a measure of freedom & detachment in so far as I'm only in India because it's a base to attack the Japs, and have no obligations or no status in 'society' & am rid of it. I see how this detachment breeds many intolerances among my friends in the regiment, how they are nasty with impatience or hatred & contempt, & how they dissipate themselves without any reference to the past or the future as though the present is an accident. And I see that this is a dangerous element. The elements are all dangerous. That's why it can be such a hell of a good play if we can tighten & shape it. It will need some pretty ruthless standardising & sharpening of characters. Will you send me your sketches – vignettes? Plan? Perhaps when we meet next we can work it out in detail: we could in Highfield. I doubt whether we could concentrate on it anywhere else.

I must go now, Frieda, to inspect rifles & oil & dry my revolver, so solong to you. I won't be long. In fact I'm not leaving you at all.

Tuesday 19th Oct.

I don't think I can write: I'm on the *Deccan Queen* returning the way you & I returned, from Bombay to Poona. The day has been beautiful through & through me & yesterday became beautiful in the late afternoon in the same way & I was rinsed with sunlight & clarity and the sensation of springtime consummated in the rare & brilliant equipoise that summer in England feels and declares for two or three days during its passage. Bombay was something lucid and responsive and various that welcomed me and led me into itself. It was drenched in the magic that was never there before: but now wherever we went there is some magic there, like the virtue that Good King Wenceslas's footsteps possessed. I'll tell you it briefly, where I went. I went from the wharf to the bank & then to a bookshop. Bought Sophocles, looked at an amusing *Cahiers des Arts* with a series of surrealist black & whites & an interplay of natural & human forms: the tree, the river = the lover, the life stream. Went to the Taj; sat by the string orchestra for lunch under the theatrical red lights: for the first time I loved it, was just tickled to death &

happy about it – red lights, fiddles, faces, all the starched military & the demi-mondain dubious citizens. Then went & read books in Thackers – read Edwin Muir's autobiography. Looked in lots of shops for an Xmas present for Gilly but Bombay has nothing I want to give to Gilly, which shows my esteem for Gilly. Well, I'd not been to Marine Drive or Hotel Marina because something deeply loving & near in me said Not Yet. But at 6 pm it said Now. I went down past Gordon's, past Maison Vienna, past Rotary International East Asia Office, past lots of places I never noticed because I was in your hand & in the cradle of your mind & enchantment sealed my forehead. The familiar waterfront & headland & sea were joyous, not a bit sad at all, but joyous. I sat opposite our window, all open, I could see the top of the wardrobe, I think it was empty. I sat on the sea wall where we often sat. I was happier than I've been since I left you. Not as happy as we were then, but very happy, though, knowing it was like that & was & was & *WAS*. My body knew it quite clearly, sitting on the sea wall & seeing the bedroom & where the bed would be between the wardrobe & the window & now, return-ing there quite simply & easily & feeling you opening and enclosing and liberating me. I keep words away from it. But you want to know how happy I was & in what way I was happy, don't you Frieda?

The urchin who said 'Taxi' wasn't there, nor anybody we know except the policeman.

In the evening I went to Menon's flat. He & Rawdon were out. I sat in the chair you sat in & I read for two hours Gertrude Stein's *Paris France*. It is a good book indeed. I was happier than I've been for months in my active mind – not my entranced mind but my thoughtful mind. She stilled me, led me, let me think, made thought solid & human for me, Gertrude Stein of all people did this for me. And your chair also. It seemed all night you were there, there was a powerful presence of you, powerful & delicate as thistledown. I never felt you weren't there. They came in at 9.30

& we ate & talked for two hours. Then I had to run. *They* talked mostly – mostly gossip about literary 'figures' – the usual slander – this time Toller, Virginia Woolf, Keynes & Lopokova & Duncan Grant & Fry. They did it kindly & I liked to listen & argue. But they haven't any roots at all, these two boys, none at all. That is obvious. They are very kind & very civilised but no peasant in them.

I was late. I missed the launch taking us back to the ship. I began talking to some Navy men, met a Welsh officer & he smuggled me onto his launch & I slept on a destroyer & they got me a launch this morning to get back to my own party. Now it's all over. They were very kind, the destroyer officers, very kind, very formal, very cautious because they live so close together in such small rooms for so long without a change, they daren't be rude to each other or scarcely be each other. I liked it there.

Today I had a lot of letters brought down by one of our drivers. Two from you. I detached myself from the throng as soon as the conference I was at finished & slipped into the swimming baths & undressed & lay in the sun to read your letters. I wanted to be naked in the sun to read them, naked & brown except for my hired bluecanvas shorts.

I've only read them once & I'm not going to answer them now. Only to say you are right & the early pages of this letter are wrong. Frieda, don't be furious with me when I get the great things in my littleness in opposition each to each. There *is* a conjunction and a resolving of greatnesses and you know it better than I do. Don't call me conscience-ridden. There's never been guilt in us, thank God, never from the beginning of time have we – you to me & I to you – had guilt. I don't know whether I'll see you before your child is born. I'm glad your body is housing him so well & glows about him. Keep him. Bear him well. I would be proud if I were – if he were – I can't say it, dearest. Sometimes I had a very bad feeling about your baby, about him being conceived. I always thought then, when it hurt me, of Philip Bossiney in *The Forsyte Saga* when he was out in the fog and Soames was lord of the earth. It is a very wrong bad wicked feeling for me, & harmful. I didn't let it stay. I couldn't help it Frieda. I had to feel it in the leaping wild panther part of me. You probably knew I felt it. It was tangible in me, a kind of forest fire on my body, on my skin a bad burn.

I had a letter from Gweno. This is a mystery I cannot comprehend, but I adore the greatness of it, of this illimitable & definite gift of love. It also frightens me. I had three letters from Michael who nearly called on Wallace in Delhi. One from Dick who is glad you & I are us now. Dick was born in heaven.

I wrote to Gilly. She will get her letter a day before this. I've been keeping this to read your letters first. Thank you for your letters, Frieda darling. I love you for ever & ever and my being quickens & becomes of worth & ability in you.

Goodbye for now, Frieda darling,

Alun

Menon & Rawdon were disappointed you weren't with me. 'She is very charming,' Rawdon said. I said only 'Frieda?' & sighed.

Late on Wednesday night:
I come to you with emotions & thoughts – & must use words that I would do without if I could come to you in silence, not through distance, as we must. Frieda, if the world *was really you* and I & not other duties & loyalties as well – Frieda, I am writing to you. It is all I can do just now, isn't it?

I have still only read your three letters once. I have thought of them incessantly & deeply. Last night I heard myself shout No No No. I tried when I heard that voice crying, I tried to find a reference – what was it denying, darling? One other night on board the ship I hadn't gone to sleep. I wanted you in the darkness, everyone else was asleep. I lay on my tummy & my hands stretched over the pillow & my fists clenched & I couldn't stop myself weeping – & there were no tears at all. It was dry weeping. And then it stopped itself & I don't remember anything, not even sleeping. I do not try to find what it means. As long as it is happening so deeply that I cannot reach it I am quiet & willing.

Your letters are a great part of you. I understand more & more: and you speak of you & me but what you say applies universally often & often. You say I was taught to live the truth & that is easier than to be taught to hide the truth. You have stirred me terribly in saying that & made me understand vast things I couldn't understand before & was worried about. The jackals are barking tonight. I could live in the darkness of tonight, the warm prettiness of the stars, the little blue darkness of the sky inlaid with patines of bright gold. Frieda, I am full of peace because of you. You will remember that, please, won't you? When I write priggish things, like saying I seek some intense & inmost tidiness of the soul, remember please I mean only that I'm gasping for somewhere I can at least & at last *breathe*. And when you accuse me, gently & with love but yet accusingly, of being delicate & cruel in my thoughts, my analysing seeking thoughts that examine a living & organic thing, don't see just that. If I *do* that, it is myself that suffers also.

You reveal yourself (or become to me, that's nearer what I mean) very many different things. Your letters humble me, intellectually, & in terms of experience. Your body does not humble me, your living presence does not humble me. Any more than being with Mair my sister. Because it is so that you are natural to me. We've always been natural to each other, perhaps for too long. You say you are such that one almighty emotion or necessity can over-ride you & that you would reject the longing the physical longing. I wouldn't reject it. I adore it. I adore it beyond all the Karmas & Nirvanas and liberations from it that the wise men praise. I never live so much as

164

then. Nothing on earth is ever so positive, so proud, so natural & dignified and vibrant as that. I have never tried to suppress it nor would I try to drown a child or refuse its eyes. I hate it unutterably when it is not an expression of love, when it is a satisfaction & not a consummation. I suppose people who live together a long time must often want only its satisfaction & that is alright because it is rhythmic & has been proved by their living together. I have never had time for that, my life hasn't been long enough. That's how it's happened to be to me, I don't *seek* the exaltation I've been trying to speak of. I don't hanker for it – except sometimes in a sort of rutting phase that I don't like but accept as it comes. – But I have known no happiness like that happiness. That is a simple observation & holds good for my 29th year. I'm not legislating!

Darling I'm conscious of more wonders moving in their own obscurities than ever before, yet I can say & write nothing. You say you re-read *Raiders' Dawn* & I wasn't a poet but your lover & they were unbearable. I'm glad I've ceased to be a poet to you. I've never been one to myself & I was frightened that you'd think of me as a poet or something unfair when I came to you first. I'm glad you don't & now never will. I'm glad I've never sought poets & writers & that my talk isn't gossip about other poets' & writers' vanities & infidelities & shams, like Menon & Rawdon who are embittered by Toller & Woolf & Auden & Lopokova. I may meet them in the course of life. That is alright. But not to *seek* them, to seek gifted men & gifted women & be cultivated by them. I want independence very much.

Each of your letters is a new experience. You yourself surpass experience and become a new simplicity only. The world is simple. It was simple on the 7th day, wasn't it, when the sun rose upon it all.

I don't want to write this letter now. People have been coming in & smoking a cigarette & talking to me and some recession has taken place. I hide & guard you always. Menon & Rawdon wanted to know who you were. I didn't tell them although I was proud of you. Alfred

Aslett asked me how I'd 'met the Aykroyds'. I said slowly 'Oh, well, we'd always known about each other, sir'. I realised after I'd said it that I'd told him the whole truth.

I want to write poetry. It would be such a relief to write. I wait & hunger for the relief & the poetry.

Have you got 'The Orange Grove' & 'Ward "o" 3 (b)'? Could you send me them if you have? And will you send me the August poems? I've no copies of 'The Map' or 'Hands' or 'What is love at best?' I would like your *Statesman* now & again, not too often; and your vitamins I'll ask you for when I need them, bless you for wanting to send them. I'll need them when I have to *carry* all the food I shall eat. I'll send some books to you & my tweed jacket when I can get a little time to find some paper & string. I've got another big exercise in a couple of days & no time even to *look* at my lake. The lake is loud, the night is cold & starry. I would I were with you, Frieda mine.

Late on Saturday night:

That is two nights have gone since I wrote last & two inordinately busy days. Nights in which I was tired & therefore chose to fulfil my duties as brother, son, what you will, and write some of the letters I owed. And tonight has, in its way, been as busy & exhausting as today. We're sweating on the top line and I find myself being given a lot of important tasks in planning and training, and my long bamboo shoot of a colonel leans pretty heavily on me at times. And of course I simply love the feeling of being consulted and trusted & expected to do things well. I find most of my satisfactions in this power-behind-the-throne complex. It was partly the same inverted vanity that made me so rudely insist that I didn't want the promotions that were dangled in Karachi – and when my report came to the unit today Gwyn came in and harangued me for being a sententious fool. 'What?' he said histrionically 'Do you honestly mean to say you want to go into action with this inept mob?' And I thought for two seconds and I looked up at him & I said 'Honestly, you bastard'. And he said, 'You're crazy'. Intellectual conversation! But it's as much service to Mammon to refuse a promotion as to take it. One can't ever be clean, perfectly pure: and one is a prig to imagine that one can. So I go my own way & don't glorify my motives. Thank Christ.

That's why I am writing to you after attending a boring hogging drink party – the Sergeants' Mess invited the Officers to a Social Evening. Imagine it. There was one funny sergeant who sang 'I'm an old cowhand on the Rio Grande' and I laughed honestly at his capers. But for the rest it was just coldly nauseating & it ended by Gwyn (the Adjutant) *ordering* the officers to go. The colonel ordered Gwyn to order us. I refused. Then Jack Gush who had three stitches in his nose this evening at a soccer match, got obstreperous, so I had to collect & soothe him & take him to bed.

And although I couldn't write to you last night when I was by myself I can write tonight when I've been in all the gawkishness of a stag party.

I came back to my lamp & its attendant mosquitoes and your letters were in my pocket all night & I've been quietly reading them & my heart saying Yes & No & Yes & No to you all the time. I had a swift dream as I read – one second perhaps – of being posted as missing believed killed & coming back & fetching you and being with you afterwards all the time and writing under a new name & living under a new name & being more intensely & completely ourselves than we could ever be before that death. And then swift as the dream came the Johnsonian NO. ABSURD. ESCAPIST. IDIOT. BAS. It was a sweet dream – like yours of scattering children like flower seeds about the world & not bothering to tend or cling to them but just letting them be. As if the world ever lets anything be. As if there is no ineluctable consequence for each action and commitment. I love the world's Greek justice and I believe in paying the piper. I want no cheap things. I can pay with everything – except sometimes with money.

I I I I I I I I I – silly word. I'm not very I, darling: it's only that I'm not objective, and events are significant only through their passage through me. It's a pity: but there it is. I've told you in every letter that I *can't* imagine you as Frieda Aykroyd despite the fact that my own eyes have seen you with Wallace & Gilly at Highfield. I can't help it. You're my woman & that's all I can feel or see. When I see the rest it's at the expense of a greater truth: it's like accepting a statistic.

Frieda, I know there's a lot of hurt ahead of us. It's trite to say so. It's so bloody obvious. I also know we are made to survive it. Perhaps I'm most 'jumpy' about the physical danger – it's like a horse race you can't guarantee a win: the rest I'm sure about. I mean that it will work out its own salvation, that is its own justice. But this desire & this love & this memory of your living presence is so powerful it forces my pen to speak of things my mind & some other queer religious part of me cannot envisage yet.

Tomorrow is Sunday. I *hope* (not too much) to get some freedom by the lake in the afternoon. Hockey match at 6. Perhaps I can write this poem that so presses in me. It would be like being in bed with you again. And that also will happen, because the desire is as vital and clean & simple as the pushing of young grass through the rainy earth

Goodnight, Frieda Buttery,
Your lover Alun Lewis

Frieda

This letter has been many things before I've started writing it. It's been all sorts of things in my mind, as you & I and Gillie and life and death and fever have been many things. I've got a nice fever tonight: I adore it. I feel hot and sometimes I'm somebody else & sometimes myself and sometimes you & I don't want to eat any food & that's a nice feeling in itself to be rid of the desire for food, to be free of enjoying meals. I'm going to sleep when I've written to you & tomorrow doesn't concern me at all: fever makes me irresponsible and natural & willing. Tomorrow's alright. I'll do it. I'll be away for three days. Thursday to Saturday – tramping the mountains of the barren sun: utter waste, utter negation, rehearsal of death, pocket of time to fall through, indifference, acceptance, endurance. That's the pattern of the strenuous existence. It's a bastard existence, I hate it, and take it with equanimity and indifference.

No letter has come from you for over a week. I haven't minded, I've not lacked you: only to the same extent as I've lacked myself. Do you *like* being each other? I know we are also ourselves, two separate historical beings, but I have this new feeling always that I can ask of you anything I can ask of myself: that if there is in me another desire or willingness or, these being absent, pure passive faith in what comes to pass, then it is also in you. Sometimes some facet in us glitters in opposition to the other in you, as if two signalling lamps should clash with each other, sending signals at the same time instead of replying to each other in turn. And it is a great freedom to live in this knowledge & to be able to look for the truth when my pen is writing to you. I've been indifferent to love this week, it began on Sunday afternoon. I could even tell you about that. I've been working pretty well all day for the last week & I haven't had any time to consider my self except when I stole two hours on Sunday afternoon. I went down to the lake and swam. On the way down through the long cotton grass whose ears are thorny parachutes that prick your ankles as you walk I aided three Indian boys in chasing an iguana. It was a beautiful beast. They had cornered it on a currant bush & I saw it break cover & I shouted & pointed to the swaying line of grass and they chased it & stoned it & killed it.

It was like killing Lawrence's snake. An obscenity. My only motive in disclosing its escape was to know what beast it was. It was a beautiful huge 3' lizard, a soft sleek brown. It body was very tranquil in death. They cut off its tail, which has an aphrodisiac secretion in a gland. I went on then to the lake where I was quite alone and stripped by the brown flood water under the bushes and let the sun smooth my body and my genitals. And my body was thinking of you and me. But my mind said very remotely, like an arbiter 'Body is captivated, but the mind is not at one with the body.' And at that antilogy the body withdrew its thoughts & its desire as if rebuked and I went & swam my body and came back wet & fishlike & insentient. You were *not* there; and my mind said it so implacably: the world has harsh and final demands which I must fulfil. The rest is not possible until the demands of the world are admitted & executed. I hate this passionately, passionately, passionately. I accept it coldly, with the calculating coolness of a man betting at the races. I hate betting at the races. But this gamble is a necessity. Damnation.

I want you to send me the negative of one of those snaps you took of me: will you please? Mother would love one more than somewhat, I know. May I borrow it to get some prints?

I am still wanting to send you books and clothes: my Kafka, two new *Horizons*, Max Beerbohm's essay, Lillian Bowes-Lyon & Robert Frost's poems, and the new unimportant poems I've written in embryo; and my tweed jacket: and there is my self waiting physically to take itself to you by some fortuitous inevitable arrangement of leaves and trains. I'm so hopelessly tied down to the battalion just now that getting free is ridiculous. I will get free. I want to get two teeth filled and can't get any time. Absurd flap of work. I think I was silly to refuse promotion. It was somehow too much for me, and too different from my impulses, and I wasn't interested in it, but only in you and in being in a job I somehow know instinctively is my job for the time being. It doesn't matter much.

Darling, this lonely love letter is all I can send. I feel very bleak and trivial ending this letter and turning to my thin bed and the cessation of one's life that sleep is. Giving myself again to tomorrow.

My love to Gillie.
And to you my self.
Do you want it? Alun.

214565 *Lt. A. Lewis*
6*th* *Bn South Wales Borderers*
ABPO 21

[October 30th]

Dear Frieda

After twelve days of nothing I received your letter – I think it's the 30th today – Saturday anyway. I've been in bed for 3 days shaking off a temp & catarrh and typing out some poems which I'm enclosing.

I'm sorry my long letter had to be how it was & you had to dig so deep & hard in replying to it. I'm sorry, because perhaps I've pestered you: and been fussy & foolishly impatient and too eager to find words and give hospitality to intuitions. I knew I was weary of the perpetual illuminations that kept everything awake & forbade any sleep. And these poems are perpetuating them to your discomfiture perhaps. But it's necessary to distinguish between me & the poems: I only want to get the poems out of me where they were so exhausting. Don't read them unless you feel sturdy enough.

It's so much better to be simple and not involved. I covet your patience, but I don't want to analyse any emotions any more. I nearly lost direction: even if I have, it's essential to become simple. And for you, & your new child.

Please congratulate Wallace: with Wavell he should be able to help mightily. The famine is world news now, thank God. Did you see LIFE on the Hot Springs Conference? It was terribly rude, mainly because the press was snubbed.

Darling, I'm very sorry, your pen never arrived. I suppose it was too tempting a little parcel for the sorters to withstand. The 30 chips did, silly billy.

Has Gilly's heather reached her? If not I'll send her one of the sprays Mother sent me at the same time. Please let me know.

I'm enclosing a letter of mother's. I thought you'd like a glimpse of her – the people she refers to in it – Johnnie is a crude little cousin, 'Aunt Lizzie's' son – we hadn't heard of him for years. Xavier is a Belgian who used to write to Mair before the war as 'pen-pal' – he escaped after June 1940 via Spain. Girlie is Mair.

Perhaps I'll allow myself to answer your letter – I hope I don't. Do I need to? Your child won't disturb: he is necessary & he is life. I shall love him.

I've got something solid in mind about the play – it's started to speak & shape *itself.* I wish we could get together over it. Must be quiet now.

Love to Gillie: Love from Alun

214565 Lt. Alun Lewis
6th Bn. South Wales Borderers
ABPO 21
Nov. 8th (Tuesday)

Frieda dearest,

It's more than a week since I wrote to you. It has seemed a long time to me and I wish I could have avoided it. I went into hospital last Monday (Oct 31) and didn't succeed in fretting and bluffing my way out of it until yesterday. I tried to write to you there but it was quite useless. I had to get out in order to live at all. I wasn't really ill: merely a temperature and a bronchial traffic jam. Despite the doctor's learned waffle about an enlarged spleen and his avid pursuit of parasites in my blood which he cozened and seduced daily with injections of adrenalin followed by pricking my finger and examining the pink results. It wasn't the doctor's fault that I had to get out of there. It was simply the lack of toughness of my mind which I'm afraid isn't half as strong as I'd hoped and has really behaved very badly of late. It has been without conversation and without solace: a kind of deliberate impoverishment of all living streams, a shrinking and a despairing. I don't know why. But I've never been so cast off, so worthless, purposeless, unresponsive. I loathed myself for it and was anxious about it, too. I think it's shredding away a bit now, the morning mist is shredding as I write from the deep lake below me in the hills. It's a long time since my ancient enemy made such a determined assault on me. Damn his bleary eyes.

When the doctor thought I had malaria he said 'That means fifteen days in bed and a fortnight's sick leave for you.' I didn't say a word, not even to myself, but despite my inner censorship some excited part of me began rushing through the possible actions of the future, catching the Madras Express, Arkonam again

& Mettupalayam & the young leaning saplings and the house high on the hill. Dearly beloved mirage of a high temperature, fading as soon as the blood returns to normal. I'd have loved to come and see you, yet somehow I never thought it would come about. Away from you I can never find the utter almost childish peace which you unfailingly give when I'm with you. When we are separated the sadness grows and we seem to be spinning one of those bitter webs of Greek legend, like traumatic subjects of a broad and indifferent destiny whose mind has long been made up.

But don't pay any attention to my morbid moods, sweet. It's mainly the hangover of physical weakness. Sometimes I cave in at the apparent sadness of existence. Again, I don't know why. The view from the hut I'm sitting in now is very very beautiful: so it is from Highfield. Why do we always pay such hard coin for delight? Like the Indian peasant whose field of millet is mortgaged to the bania. There must be something very wrong about humanity, mustn't there, to make such turgid muddles.

I'm almost alone in camp: the only other officer is the padre, a little bandy north country man who has been ten years in India, most of the time with a phoney mission in Central Provinces. He is really doing very little with us either, for our mood has no religion in it, and we sheer away from any clericalism or confessional advances. Yet he's quite a happy complacent little squirrel of a man. Time doesn't seem to gnaw and gore him as it does me. Tell me, Frieda, should I be lighthearted and confident of the goodness of things or am I being quite sensible when I feel grave and badly troubled? I suppose it depends on what level one is living, doesn't it? I only know that one is happiest without thinking, and one is oneself in feeling only.

I came back yesterday evening to camp. Old Harry Tudor was here with his bald head and bought me a thick sandwich of bread & tomato & curry from the canteen & an enamel mug of chah for supper. I sat at my improvised table for hours, from dusk to midnight, wrestling with poetry, achieving something *perhaps*, but no satisfaction. Writing poetry does not satisfy, it exhausts. I don't know when one experiences pleasure: there is no place for pleasure in the process of writing poetry as far as I can see: yet one would rather write poetry than do anything else on earth. Strange, isn't it? But there are few creative processes which have a positive content of joy. Love seems to have it all far far more than its share. And yet, perhaps not. Love has more than its share of tragedy too.

I've been reading Zola's *Germinal* with absorbing excitement. It's good to read a great book, isn't it? I'm so caught by it that I bought Dostoevsky's *Crime and Punishment* in Poona yesterday to live with another great book when I've finished with Zola's dreadful awe-inspiring coal mine. To write with such simple sincerity and to be at such pains to state the ugly truth of it all is an act of devotion to life.

I spent a couple of hours in the bookshop in Poona yesterday and read some more of Verrier Elwin's *Leaves from the Jungle*. Do you know him? He's a missionary among the Gonds. I'd like to meet him very very much. He is without cant and without religious pretentiousness, he has the laugh of a centaur and isn't perturbed by the horrible diseases of his people. He's published a book of Indian folk songs and also edits a quarterly called *Man in India* something after Frazer's *Golden Bough* in its approach. I've subscribed to it & will send it to you if you like. How attractive the thought is of committing oneself to such a wild and austere field of study and roughing it out till the crack of doom among those simple primitives. There was a nice book on British painting by John Piper, too, which I revelled in; and a too expensive but splendid collection of Robert Graves's poems.

I read Lewis Carroll's *Hunting of the Snark* in bed last week and saved myself for a whole morning by writing a long and silly scroll in the same vein concerning the Hunting of Tojo. I'll copy it out one day and send it to Gilly. If I could decorate it it would be fun, but I've got no gift for drawing things fantastic, like the snail you drew for me in a letter once. I loved that snail more than any snail I've met. Even John Clare's 'frail brother of the morn'.

I'm very sorry your dear gift of the fountain pen failed to reach me. You mustn't send anything small & tempting by post: it's too risky, isn't it? I'm very sorry, Frieda. But this little platignum that Dick bought me when I bust my jaw is writing quite nicely. And will see me through the short period of semi-civilised living that remains. I won't need a good pen for a good time.

Well, my fair lady, the morning passes away and I want to try my hand again at a jagged story. I tried in vain to type some approaches to the play. I think things are too hot & immediate – for *me* at least. Perhaps you have them more objectively grouped.

Tell me when you are going to Telacheri – is that the way to spell the lovely sounding name of it? I'm afraid I'll get no Xmas leave at all. Sad.

My love to Gilly & Wallace; be patient & kind to yourself, Frieda. And this is from   Alun

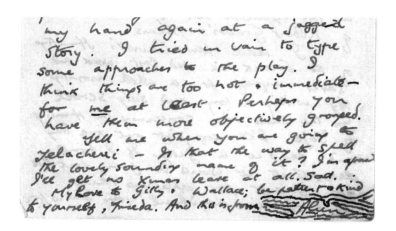

214565 Lt. A. Lewis
6th Bn. South Wales Borderers
A.B.P.O. 21

Nov. 14th

Frieda dearest,

It's Sunday night. I want this to reach you before you go to Tuticorin (I can't tell whether your letter says the 20th or the 26th) and I want it to go on the journey with you & Gilly instead of me – no, *as* me. I'm very far away from you – do you mind if I quote a poem I wrote the last winter I was in England? It always soothes me.

> Absence & distance soft as snowflakes fall
> In long silk skeins on this unearthly night,
> Effacing and gathering up all that resists.
> Somewhere your curtain falls against the light.

Oh Frieda, did you hear me sigh then? Can you feel the leadenness, the persistent oppression that I'm trying & trying to accept & wear and hide? Oh dear, a cri de coeur on page 1! Too soon, child, too soon. But if I could put my head on your shoulder with my cheek against the warmth & welcome of your breast – and rest rest rest.

I try to look at myself obliquely & analyse it down to something rational & explicable. I say 'It's because you've been three years in the Army & *it* still delays & doesn't happen & you go on waiting & waiting & naturally you get a bit rotten & downcast.' Then when that fails to help I make myself go more fully into the other things – go & watch A Company playing B Company at Soccer, or go & umpire a hockey match, or go & play some records in the reading room or go & talk to somebody. But I really think that I am escaping not resolving the trouble by doing that. It's in my head & in my heart: & I can't help it being there. It's not malignant sometimes, for years. Then it becomes a force in me, disrupting and corroding, & I've got a real fight then. It's always manifested itself in an intense awareness of the *waste* that I'm causing or suffering: Today has been wasted in me, Now is wasting away in me. It's a debt I can never make good, the expense of Now wasted away in me. And what is waste? I think it's the feeling of dissatisfaction with one's deeds, the feeling of incompetence, of being hustled into inefficiency by the daily rush of trifles & duties, none of which give any feeling of accomplishment or fulfilment. I sometimes reach an equipoise where I say 'STOP' – & the rush of disappointment & worrying stops like a flow of traffic held up by a policeman: & I say to myself 'You've wasted lots of time in the past in this same soul-destroying way: yet you emerged, child, and the strength & love in things & people came back into you & you were alright again. It won't last for ever: it's only the same old bother: it'll go.' And I say Yes, it'll go. And then the traffic starts flowing again & it's all I can do not to cry out with sorrow & hurt. At other times in these long inadequacies I suffer I think I want it to go a little further, a little further, that I might explore the fields of insanity. That is a temptation that attracts & repels with like force & I don't act towards it: it's just a thought in me, not an impulse. I know it's danger: but it's very closely connected with the bit of poetry there is in me, the writing & creating mystery that wants to break down the last barriers and explore the deep involutions of trouble and complexity & relationship of things. But I don't really know whether the great poems were really written in madness. I think they were written in intervals of sanity. Madness I fear is chaos, a greater bewilderment, a worse darkness. Has any apprehension of the mystery of everything and the mystic varieties & interconnexions of the universe ever come to anybody except in a moment of exalted lucidity? I don't know.

I don't know my family antecedents: I don't know whether my great great grandfather or my maternal great uncle had moods of darkness: they say the Welsh are more prone to depression, but I see it as more in the writers of all countries than anywhere else & I think it's a disease that poets are prone to: I don't think it's a matter of race or blood: as far as I'm concerned I know I have to allow for it – and allow a great deal. I've been watching myself like a wise doctor: and last Wednesday, after I'd posted my letter to you, I was unwilling to let my mind go rushing off into another dither of self-chastisement. So I dressed up in my heavy boots & anklets & overalls, put on my kit, took a bamboo staff, & set off with a waterbottle to cross the mountains & find the battalion which was out on exercises for the week. I put a blanket & groundsheet & mosquito net in a truck that was going out there & I set off on foot just after noon. I walked slowly & steadily, feeling quietly for a rhythm to overcome the physical weakness of the touch of bronchitis I'd been in dock with. And as I followed the tracks, the bunds, the landmarks, made the pass, crossed to the next village, & the next, found the motor road & the main pass, wound down the defile and across the plain, struck across the sloping heath to the Mula river, & so on, I felt my mind submitting to the smooth & constant effort of my body till a gentle & tranquil harmony grew up between mind, body, sun & earth. Thirsty, I drank water & was satisfied. Hot, I sat under trees & was cooled by my own sweat growing cold on my overalls. Needing to reach the battalion before dusk I pushed on & the distance grew behind me and eventually I arrived. They were all bivouaced on a slope above a river which ran into a lazy pool below a broken bridge: herons stood in the long grass unperturbed by the sunburnt soldiers bathing & swearing & laughing in the pani, as they say. I was tired out & triumphant. Just for that day at least I'd made things better than they'd been. I stayed with them till we marched back to camp by night under the full moon of the week end. It was a lovely walk back, just in itself it was satisfying and sufficient. The earth was like a warm cheek, breath of warmth in the hay cocks, coolness turning sharp & bracing in the air, stars growing brighter in the blue night of the sky, boots going on & on tranquilly, and all I was saying at all was, Is this the direction? Which of these tracks is the right one? How do we cross this rocky nullah? And once I'd solved each little question there was nothing to do except walk on across the next strip of moon-green. And it's been Saturday and Sunday, & tomorrow we start the old round again. I've done nothing & can do nothing yet. A half-finished story, four unnecessary poems & nothing else to show the black journeys that were made.

Frieda, I'm not writing all this to depress you or myself, or to ask you for strength or patience: I'm only just telling you so that you'll know, dear. You *will* know, of course you know. It's always been like this on earth, hasn't it? Absence & distance . . . . . .

Your lovely long letter I received on Friday: it had gone looking for me in hospital & at camp & so it didn't find me until after I'd received the poems & the negatives & the *Statesman* & the three stories. Thank you for sending me all these things. I've sent you two *Horizons* & Max Beerbohm's essay on Lytton Strachey, the kerosene having evaporated now. And I've returned 'Stones for Bread' because Dick sent me his copy. I've been reading the poems in your handwriting quietly & they've been very sweet to me, very gentle and good. It's easier to understand the necessity of pain when you find your own heart has guessed at it in the beginning and put it into words with such dignity & music as it was capable of attaining. They make a testimony for me that I wouldn't do without. Whether the unwritten unachieved poems come or not, there is at least this, which is true. I don't think of them as poems: I shouldn't have shown them to Michael: he could only consider them as poems. Essentially they are not 'poems': they are a communication between you and me.

Frieda, this letter is so unlike yours that I wonder whether you'll be hurt. I can only reply to your letter in silence: my truest answer is the one that I would make to flow round you, silently. There are some answers which need words, but I'm reluctant to give them words. You say that whatever happens or is said, the happiness is ultimate and is greater than the rest and will survive them all. When you say that I hide it away in me, hide it and do not speculate or question or even contemplate it: one day it will surge up in me, when perhaps I am in some way worthy of it and then my heart will rejoice and be exceeding glad. Now I cherish it away where it can come to no harm.

You were afraid of something that might turn into resentment in me: and of something in me that in cowardice and for peace of mind would shut away this love, this burning image and deep reflection of you in me & in the world. But it would only happen like that if I died also within myself: and I need to be as terrified of that as you, or more than you. But I don't believe it at all. Many things may happen to us, but nothing that can trap and destroy the – the what? The freedom of heaven & earth & time. Isn't that what we apprehended? I know how I lose & fail back into time & the impotence of time: but I don't think these small stumblings & wounds & disasters in time can really matter much one way or the other to that great freedom that one can only leave alone. Because it IS. That's all. It IS. Thank God we can't make or mar it but that it IS & not sometimes also. You more than me. But there could be no resentment.

Perhaps I'm bunking the lesser issue. Perhaps deliberately. I don't know what will happen. In a way I've lost a stability and simplicity I had before: for I'm more lonely, less dependent & less able to depend. I know I've re-entered the wilderness. I know it when I wake, every time I wake something is reluctant & uneasy in me because the wilderness is all about. But it's the hard way of truth & I know it is all necessary & I go as best I can. And I obey you as much as I can when you say 'Let be'. 'There is so much time' you say 'please let it *be*.' I try to. So long as I don't shelve a problem, but rather live it quietly, let it grow & let it take its shape. As you your child. I want you to have months of quietness to let it grow. And the hurt of labour, oh Frieda, that too. You know that too. It won't be the same emotion as I shall have sooner or later. It won't have the same emptiness, nor the same deadness, nor the same outrage. Surely it won't, your pain is life-making, making way for more life? Sometimes I feel as if I had gone into you. And I wish it were me that you will suckle and help & fledge & fortify & send out. Life is itself. I only guess at it and wonder & wonder & wonder. At its power, its waste & malevolence, its beauty & its flooding gifts. And if I fail, it is still itself. And if I try & try, and my failures are forgiven me, perhaps I will still make something of it.

Dear love, goodnight & god bless you & make you.
Another sigh,
X X X X   Alun

214565 Lt. A. Lewis
6th Bn. South Wales Borderers
ABPO 21

Nov. 22nd Monday

Frieda

Perhaps a week has gone since I wrote: do you mind? Somehow I have been letting it be as you wished. Now it's midnight & across the lake a sentry strikes an iron bar the way they do at sea – twelve bells: the dog watch is at hand. And I am fortunate in a hurricane lamp, a low little camp table that makes me roundshouldered, a bed & a mosquito net, a sewn up sheet to slide into naked & sleep without dream and wake with a deep reluctance to a day whose ordinary duties are as slow as the clock's hand.

I wrote a poem the other night – not a poem either. Twelve lines, not really mine but only a little search in me for what has buried itself deep in the mould & the thickets of circumstance & will not easily emerge. I must leave poetry outside myself when I am not writing it. It's not me at all, not tedious fatigable me. Here are two lines for Gilly by Robert Frost

> We dance round in a ring and suppose
> While the Secret sits in the middle and knows.

Here are my twelve lines:

> Where aloneness fiercely
> Trumpets the unsounded night
> And the silence surges higher
> Than hands' or song's or mountain's height,
> I the deep shaft sinking
> Destroy the obdurate alone,
> While with a willing anguish
> You grow about me, flesh and bone.

The wild beast in the cave
Is all our pride: and cannot be
Again until the world's blind travail
Breaks in crimson flower from the tree
I am, in thee.*

Frieda, it's so hard to think of you packing your & Gilly's clothes, laying your diaphanous dust cover over, taking the train to the sands, the warm sea. I know I would be 'joyous' if I came. Looking at your photograph of me I was amazed at the absence of preoccupation in me.

I would break out of all this to you. Instead I am going to sleep myself into tomorrow.

Goodnight darling. I hope you are well.

My love,
Alun

* This is a variant of 'A Fragment', which is reproduced here in full on pages 25–6, and on page 161 of *Collected Poems*.

Nov. 26th

*My love to Gilly. I'll be
in the wilds all next week.
I'll send you an Xmas
stocking when I get back.*

*214565 Lt. A. Lewis
6th Bn. South Wales Borderers.
ABPO 21*

Frieda dearest,

I had your letter of the 21st this evening and hastily & happily put it in my shirt pocket and went down to the lake in the last hour of daylight & lay on the little landing stage that has a notice LANDING STAGE OFFICERS ONLY, and lay there reading your letter & your poems quietly and blessedly till a motor boat chugged up & emptied out two prim middle aged ladies, a pom, a captain with a map case & nobody else. They looked down their noses at me, stepped over my indolent body, appeared sorry that they couldn't rebuke me for not wearing a bathing costume & climbed the hill to the 'married quarters'. What dreadful visions those two words evoke in me – the slums of Aldershot, the horrid brick red semi-detached streets of Colchester or Brecon or any regimental depot where the wives gather in slander, the wooden gipsy huts draped in hollyhocks & washing of Bovington – the Army has coped with marriage about as effectively as with pensions and allowances: if anything survives it proves itself invincible. But I've gone a long way from the lake and the sunset and your letter. And yet, perhaps not. Frieda thank you for your letter. It's a great event when I get one from you and it sustains and wakens me like a dragonfly drying and flexing itself. I've been wandering in tedious unrhythmic circles & spirals in the wilderness of the last few weeks. Oh Christ, I want to be with you in Tuticorin. Oh how much!

I have been leaning on you, evidently. You had to reassure me, hadn't you? I'm sorry, darling. I love to lie, just before going to sleep out on an exercise, consider the stars amply and equally, and some free voice in me says in equipoise 'Frieda'. It says it so tranquilly, freely, easily – neither passionless nor muted by passion, but as if something has been inherited and is being used according to its true nature. When it is like that it doesn't matter that we have no idea what will happen: it's the simple existence of us that speaks – it doesn't even make a sentence – no verb or object in it. It isn't often like that, nor could it be, me being such dross, but as long as it's sometimes I'll be alright. It will happen next week also when we are lying among sand dunes, free as the wind that blows us to sleep. But this closed regimented camp life is abomination. I shall be glad to be rid of the battalion I couldn't bring myself to leave.

And your poems spoke to me so well, they were so familiar & in my head & in my heart. I'm very glad you sent them – they're more than the silver box that you threw away even. One day you'll give me a plain ring, won't you? I'll be able to feel it with my fingers at night in the dark & when I'm speaking to somebody else I'll be able to turn it round casually & know it.

I'm glad you like Mother, ça me fait plaisir. We've got on best together since I 'grew up' – I wasn't aware of her before. Huw is the same: since he went to college he's been as thick as thieves with mother; every morning while she made the beds he followed her from bedroom to bedroom, telling her endless anecdotes about 'Coll' and 'Rugger'; she was bored by them but loved it. And Mair was always on edge against her until she went away to College & they are very good friends now: it's rather strange, that: it isn't that she ever wanted to know or direct or interrupt, but perhaps somehow she herself is a little de trop, she extends too much in the family for there not to be a little friction when we're all together over years. This is just guessing. I've not thought about it. Daddy is the rock of love, she's the wind about it. He would grieve but not break. She would be desperate. He's been very good to us always,

always, but sometimes he was too stolid for mother. I knew all that since very early, long before I knew anything about sex.

I sent you a letter several days bye with a dark little song in it – & found it today still in a drawer. I felt very crestfallen & angry at the careless delay. I'm sorry, Frieda.

I'm not going to worry about your child and your tummy any more than I'm worried about the end of life. Because I'm wonderfully certain your little child will be born and you'll have him. I have to sigh again. Lucky sigh. And another – I feel out of breath. I can't say anything about him, except that the first sight of him will be a very great delight for me and in some mysterious way a fulfilment. I wonder whether he'll be dark or fair, whether he'll write or play the piano or be interested in things growing and changing. When will I come & see you? In July? A whole year? Highfield is very safe in me, very clear – not the safeness of an embalming, but the clarity of a spring day that so enters you with vital impressions that it cannot fade.

I share a tent with a tubby tough ex-sergeant major with a frontier medal and an army mind. He's got a tin & he's piddling into it. It's midnight & he makes an awful loud noise. He spits through the window now cleaning his teeth. Somebody's talking in another hut, a lorry is passing up the camp road, the donkey engine pumps water chuff chuff chuff chuff from the lake, the crickets are like a persistent electric twitch. Let them all be.

I'm thinking on a third tack just nowadays of yet another story. I don't think I'll try it: it's long & hard & risky: it can easily end as the last two did: become impossible & inactive half way through. It's not morbid though, which is a good thought. Nor too cynical – but to be balanced one must be satirical, that's certain. I saw a lot of people in the battalion the other midnight with a clear & satiric vision, & I drew them into words and thought 'I can make much of this'. I've been reading Graham Greene's *England Made Me*. It's good in his way, but a bit Virginia Woolf – impressionist entirely, but the impressions have a resonance & reference that make a complete case against the civilisation we permit & obey: I always think of Greene as a poet who decided to get his copy from the *Daily Mirror*. So he becomes a satirist with an exquisite sense of moments.

I went to a concert tonight: there's been a glut of them – three in a week, one has to go. They're very banal, these variety things, the 'actors' are all 'professionals', hard humourless faces, harsh voices, borrowed jokes. Officers have front seats. I sit & watch the creases in the blouses, the weak chins, the blue eyelids, the fume of dust rising from the floorboards under the tap-dancers; dirty joke follows dirty joke, a girl raises a roar that is for her body not her talent, two Indian comedians with charcoaled faces go maudlin about dear old Dixie, somebody says 'Let it go, boys, swing it' & a dreadful American flood of slush surges out of the saxophones. I can't think of a better proof of things being wrong and rotten than an Indian band swinging it. 'Lama sabacchthani?' Fancy India going the way of America. I suppose China will, too: & then we'll corrupt the Japs with swing as they corrupt the Manchurians with opium. Ça ne fait rien. Max Beerbohm is aesthetically correct in all he says. But politically the world is dead serious & fundamental & Max isn't anywhere at all, he's scarcely thought about it, it seems to me. He's just given it up & accepted his annuity. Which is a sensible thing to do.

I've lost Menon & Rawdon's address: but if you send it c/o Miss S. Sobhani, All India Radio, Bombay, it will do well enough. I don't want to go to Bombay again except you come too. I can see & smell & feel those lotuses so vividly. But the other flowers – what colour were they? I can't see them at all. That lifetime took such swift steps to hide and consolidate itself in me. I'm only just beginning to belong to it. It's only now beginning to be safe in me. The safest part of all is the nearest part. I want it again, quietly & strongly.

Everything here is a denial of it. But we must let it be, let it be.

Reading your poems now as I think of sleep some lines leap out

> Gentleness turns revealing
> A brutal face ——

This is what one always has terror of, isn't it? It can happen so swiftly and inadvertibly. The little poem means most to me, I am calmed & excited together by

> That great coldly flashing star.

The Arkonam piece would I think be more effective as a prose piece, it's so built on observation of details that yet aren't as resonant or evocative as poetry needs. The Tea Gardens you must cut down a lot: the planter is sufficiently clear in the last six lines to dispense with the escapist fantasy altogether.

> And pick pick pick pick
> Two leaves and a bud

Needs a brief concise crystalline setting rather than a long descriptive one. May I say this? It won't stop you sending more, will it?

Are you, darling, as simple as certainty? Neither you nor Gilly. Nor do you need to be. In the mirror once you looked as simple & beautiful as a sunflower. But unassailable & fragile, intangible. I wouldn't either complicate or simplify you, even if I could. Frieda, Frieda.

I will try this third story. What is there to lose? I can stand an infinite series of failures, and time can be found. Otherwise I am doing nothing except, read, write letters, sit & think, worry, do odd jobs, wait for the pistol. Only I feel I'm rushing it.

Robert Graves read my poems & sent Gweno a detailed criticism. She's sending it on to me with the poems I haven't already got out here. I don't think I've got copies of the ones I left with you – the typed ones – so could you let me have them after Xmas for long enough to read them against his remarks. I was relieved & surprised that he insists on them being published. I'd lost any belief in them I may have had. I feel all the time that I'm either washed out or waiting to start. It may be either. I'm waiting to see. It's boring, being nothing. And I am nothing here somehow. Nothing of any importance at all. I want to get away. Only I'm willing to wait & waste time if I can be with them on the day, just to be with them on the day. I'll be stabilised that day. I'll be able to write & talk & think when I've proved that. Jack Gush just walked in, ruffled my hair & said 'Goodnight son'.

Goodnight, Frieda dearest,

Love

Alun

I was in Bombay for four hours
last week: I went to the
Bristol Grill for dinner: the
chichis & the doughboys
jitterbugging. I went to no
other place of ours.

214565 Lt. A. Lewis
6th Bn South Wales Borderers
ABPO 21

Dec 7th

My dear Frieda

It's a long way today. I've been sitting at my lamp with the moon like snow and the lovely English-seeming cold moving at my back and somehow or other it seems a long way. I've written to Auntie Con, & Dick, and an old friend who suddenly wrote to me from the N.W. Frontier having seen my Manuel story in Lilliput at Abbotabad, & sent an Xmas card to Gillie, and to Mr & Mrs W Aykroyd, and Miss Sophie Sobhani and Michael. And in a neighbouring tent a little schoolboy subaltern is arguing with the doctor about rape and American soldiers in Wales and my fellow denizen, the little fat captain is groaning over his duty letter to his missus. And it seems a long way because I'm far away in nowhere & no compass could locate the way I got here. And this ghostly little Xmas makes odd little efforts to persuade me of its bounty & forethought & charity – a little tin from Gweno with a new pipe and a sweet little white sea shell from Aberystwyth & a hairpin for luck. A little book on Wales in the same series as the one I sent you – but a bad book with very ordinary colour prints – I could have made an infinitely more distinguished selection – nothing by Turner or David Jones or Augustus John. This from mother 'with love from Daddy & Girlie & me'. And these two little presents are real company to me, like Pico. Funny.

I've not heard from you since your letter with the poems. So I reread that instead. I don't need many letters from you, Frieda. One can last me a long time. It doesn't give up its entire meaning in one reading or three. I'm keeping the poems, please, for a while more.

One of them I want to keep for ever. The coldly flashing one. Poetry is a strange mystery. Strange and elusive and variable as a living person is. Sometimes meaning nothing, sometimes completely taking the mind & the heart with a power that is beyond the words altogether but is evoked by them when it chooses to be. It tantalises me, this skittishness of power. I am without it nowadays, yet I am constantly aware of it and aware of how close & yet unseizable it lies. (It *is* cold tonight: I've just put a vest on under my bush shirt & tied a green hankie round my neck.) And I'm economical & unwilling in my efforts, & uncommunicative in talk, waiting for something to move & to emerge. It's silly to wait though: I know it will probably come bubbling out in the middle of a great rush & bother of other things. I'm not a partisan of waiting; being not old enough to know that time must often be permitted to pass.

I had a nice letter from my sister yesterday with a long poem on Van Gogh she'd written in bed with flu in Manchester. It wasn't a good poem, but the last lines had something ineluctable & very real & true in them: after talking of the dullness of many lives she says of herself:

> When I feel
> The singing beauty
> Of a dreaming day
> Fill my earthen heart
> With nectar & with dew,
> I know that in the burn
> Of an artist's blood
> My ultimate desire
> Was mirrored
> Long ago

The longing for – oh what? Where? Is it – ever – really? Yes, but never for ever.

193

I've had a very military week on manoeuvres. I think I could profit from your pollen vitamin packets when I do the next one. Not that it was unduly exacting. I find it exhilarating in many ways. When I'm 'in the field' I find it incredibly easy to take a decision or make a judgement swiftly. I don't shilly shally about the implications and alternatives. I see them, weigh them & discard them in one movement of the brain & then I'm ready to carry out my decision. It's a greater accession of self reliance than I possess at normal times, because normally I am continually widening the horizon & multiplying the possibilities & breaking down the apparent simplicities into their components. I often wish I was plowing a field or breaking stones instead. It would be awful to become unreal, Frieda, wouldn't it? There are so many unreal people about already. The big business men, the big statesmen & labour leaders – they're all puppets of the forces they symbolise. The real people seem to have avoided power because they felt instinctively how inimical it is. Although Max Beerbohm deplores the century of the common man, it is the common man who is the last repository of worth – not in the mass for then he becomes a blind force: but in himself – helpless in political terms, but inestimably worth the world in himself. Women have more of it then men: so they quietly bear children as & when they can while the man destroys in mass the individuals the women are always tirelessly making. And failure? Not the crash of defeat or insolvency at all: but the harshness of success, the standardisation of the conformist. Graham Greene loves to write of the powerful man, whether he's a race gang boss or an international financier: and his whole theme is the failure he finds & fixes like a curious insect in the great & the small. It's the macabre element he finds in it that gives him distinction. I enjoy the macabre gift when it's used to analyse & elucidate the ordinary: when it's simply a goose-flesh thrill like Poe it doesn't matter one way or the other. I've tried to avoid the gruesome in life, but I suppose if I'm going anywhere I'm going towards it. That's why I get this chilly premonition of distance; I want to break out of it like a clown through a paper hoop. Break out of this into that – will it be the same each side like the clown's hoop, or amazingly different like the chrysalid & the butterfly? Dis donc. Do you know where it is going, Frieda?

It's late, too; the night is waking up. The schoolboy is talking about Bren guns now. I wish he'd go to bed. I don't like his bumptious raw voice. I played 'Una Furtiva Lacrima' tonight & Franck's *Variations Symphoniques*. What shall I do with the letters you've sent me if we go away? Shall I burn them or send them to you? I want to keep them, but I can't very well, you know.

I want to meet you so badly: so much I want the comfort of being with you. I don't suppose we'll be able to: and then it'll be not till June, July, August – when? when? And you'll be with a child in your arms. Strange world. I would have liked————

Now I'm going to sleep soon. I must let go of today now, let it go. I don't want to. I want to mark each day with my nails or my lips, but I have to let them go as they came, these days. The bullock carts creak past. It's too cold for the drivers to sleep tonight. Have you read *Don Gesualdo* yet? I've been reading some Kipling, but I find him false to India; hopelessly false but extremely necessary. People out here couldn't live on E. M. Forster – Kipling is like a peg.

> Goodnight, Frieda dearest
> In the safe wilderness
> My love by yours,
>
> Alun

[The first part of this letter is missing.]

And now after a day's dusty speeding I'm back in camp again, ready to sleep for six hours before marching out at dawn on a four day exercise: it's an absurd life: nomad, restless, like listening to jazz all the time and 'having no time for' chamber music. But as one has no choice one flows. I've got your Xmas parcel still locked away, & I'll not open it till Xmas day. It's the only real Xmas present I'll have, & it will symbolise 29 years of gifts and love. Thank you, Frieda. And the ring – it sounds lovely & is a signal honour. Will you keep it till I come & see you again, and put it on my finger that day yourself? I'd prefer. And may I come & see you any time? *Please.*

The journey was very dull: I was continually nodding & eating bananas and talking small beer with Crewe -Read who is as comfortable a soul as a hot water bottle. I was thinking about the story I wrote during the week three midnights running, and I could see how it had trailed off & become insignificant. I think it's a lack of spiritual energy in me. The incident I was trying to write round was significant – but a desire to finish the story quickly, plus a hesitation about the censor, plus a blinkering of the vision (I'm more & more aware of the blinkers I wear) made it more & more trivial. It was based on the weekend I spent with my brother Glyn at Poona last Saturday. We stayed at the Napier – Glyn is a private soldier and has had a dirty uncomfortable life out here. He'd just come from the other side of India – six days in a fanless 3rd compartment with a wooden rack to sleep on – & no hot meals. He sat in the awful dressed up dining hall of the Napier in his cheap 'issue' shirt & too-small trousers, and he slept like a breast fed baby in the sheets – the first 'bed' he's slept in since he left home. There was a terrific gin party in the next room – some very drunk & noisy officers singing cheap songs: I went in there at 2 am after they'd thrown the hotel manager out & told them to shut up or – Well the

Poona scene *is* significant. And my relations with Glyn are so, too. His world & mine have become so different – & I had every thing a writer wants in contrast, social implications, decline & fall of empires & individuals – every thing except character. I couldn't create character: and that is due to lack of energy in me – just like a woman can't create a child sometimes. So the story must wait & be rewritten. I'm sorry I'm so dull. It's expensive.

But I'm resting in a deep sense, too. I'm more relaxed & less agitated, about our personal fates & interdependences. And I can find you now whenever I have peace, without worry or complexity. And you are very beautiful to find and very young and mature and exciting to love – although there are hundreds of dusty miles between us. Perhaps we'll meet – maybe in February or March – would you mind?

Goodnight darling.
My love to you,
Alun

Frieda, Frieda,

Evening: evening in the jungle; our car parked by the roadside, a lamp tied to the vines, a fire of dead wood blazing in a trench, our bodies clean after swimming and placid after eating, the night very quiet, scarcely any insect violence or insistence, voices sounding tranquil: and all the life that hides away emerges and makes memory natural & immediate and communication with one not here oh so much easier than at other times. I've got your unanswered letter in my head, and if it asked for a reply I would answer it, but it didn't. It said something, and wanted no more from me than also to say something. I say only Frieda, Frieda, and many things that happened to us are happening again, in this liberation of the Indian jungle, in me. The element in me that nags and vitiates is absent. I'm simple again, & like a stream, it may be deep, it may be still or swift, it has its own nature. Oh God, how lovely it is, this interim of peace. I looked at a big map of India yesterday as we travelled down here & I found Tuticorin, and Tinevelly and Madura. And Telacheri & Nagercoil – and so again your name was written on the map. I'm only writing this note in my staff diary to tell you so.

When one feels like this thought processes seem to be superseded by a more spontaneous system – sense impressions, a succession of flashes on the photographic plates of the brain. I saw you with an amazingly natural immediacy in your yellow frock and your heaped bushels of fair hair at Victoria Terminus Bombay and I felt exactly the same sensitive communications of a trouble I knew instinctively I could soothe and a birdlike wildness I knew at once would furl its wings and nest with me. And you then and I then were free of all complexities; and everything to which we belonged, and which had shaped us, & to which we owed ourselves fell away, ceasing to perturb us with the strained phantasies of uncertainty. I haven't written before because I've been busy & trivial & boring and didn't want to prate to you like the harassed subaltern I was. It's interesting to wonder how much a bad mood is made from pettiness, how much from some cosmic foreboding. Both were present in me and both have momentarily lifted. I was very conscious of the hotchpotch we make of life in an Army, the bad way we do a lot of jobs because we're doing them all at the same time and for a purpose that is intolerable. And I had a wicked sense of dissatisfaction with everything I put my hand to, & in consequence did them worse than I needed to, because I had no faith in myself doing them. And I'm clumsy & dreamy in matters of memory & administration. I forget details or slur them, and condemn myself like a Dickensian Bumble. And the whole vast enterprise the world is engaged on falls into doubt in me and I go under a surge of bungled violence & released irresponsible harm. Have you ever heard a battery of artillery laying down a barrage of shell? It's a terrible experience philosophically & morally, all that crushing dreadful arbitrary violence. Physically it's just a bloody row & a reflex fear or shudder. But to think of the impersonal evil it implies is terrible. And being out here in the jungle is to be away from all that. Here there are bamboos curved from the centre of each clump like arches leaping from the columns of the nave. Villages simple & solitary in clearings isolated completely and it seems eternally from all our obligations & distractions. Pools which please the cattle and refresh my own dusty naked body. Dry brushwood to brew tea & fry eggs & boil potatoes & try out a pancake. We crossed a belt of jungle on foot this morning, I with the compass, & Crewe-Read with his shotgun. We saw two 'cheetals' (?) – like gazelles – but he wouldn't shoot them. Then I started a huge snake & we chased it. It was very beautiful and fine, its head raised above the low grass, swift & sinuous. He shot three times. When he hit it it curled up slowly, keeping its head raised above its circled dying body, & its narrow fierce little head stared at us fixedly. We killed it with a stick. Killing it seemed natural, too.

I would like this to get to you by Xmas, but I don't think it will. Tinevelly is a long way away. It must have been a bad journey – and little Lacquer* getting lost. I'm very glad she was returned to you. Poor Gilly. Like the heather, only much much worse.

Three nights later
I've been holding this in the vain hope I'd hear from you. Nothing at all at all. Why can't you write to me, Frieda? I wish you were able to. It's so necessary to me.

I'm back with the battalion again and maybe I'll write you another letter or two. Things are like a railway terminus here – I don't know which platform or which time. I'll write you an 'ordinary' letter next week. I did so want to come & stay with you. I'm getting fatalistic: indeed impatient to have a showdown with fate. I've lived a queer unnatural life these last three years. I depend far more than I like upon the simple physical excitement of movement and newness – for instance I rode the motor bike back from the jungle – 250 miles – at an absurdly fast pace and was yet perpetually aware of the hills, the land, the earth of the road, the peasants, the funerals & markets and oxen and crops. I was exhilarated and tireless, and just balancing always the equation of safety & speed. It's not good for me: I pay for it. I've paid for it these two days since I arrived – a nervous depressive dissatisfaction which turns furiously & cruelly upon myself. I am my own scapegoat.

Mother's Xmas letter came today. It was a lovely letter. Shall I send it to you? Do you mind?

* the family cat

Frieda, make a great effort to write to me, *please*. You keep me company not in what you are doing now but in Bombay and in July. The first evening when someone called to take you (me thrown in) to Gloria's dinner party, I remember the spontaneous unquestioning feeling I had that the man who called was from outside and that it had happened to us & we didn't belong except to each other. A marvellous feeling of blood relationship, not then of a lover (but of a brother, not only a brother): and I'll always have that, though there are so many imponderable antagonistic forces and so many weaknesses in me that prevent & prevent. I wish I hadn't this capacity for pain. It so wearies me. I wish I was strong like oak. And less aware of the waste & the going wrong of things and mea culpa in it all. But not in us.

Last night I sat in an hotel lounge by myself with you & watched the people & blew lazy smoke rings and was very very happy and secretly alive.

But the great need now is to be patient & to endure.

Be patient & endure, Frieda. And you too Alun.

Goodnight darling and please also kiss Gillie
My love to you you you
Ever
Alun

P.S. I may get leave FEBRUARY. Can I come?

[The first part of this letter is missing.]

. . . ritual. On Saturday night Gush & I stood for an hour under the bo tree while they chanted & beat their tympani in the bare little temple. Two dusky rows of jungle boys against each wall and a cup of oil burning in front of Gumpati. The chants & the beating slowly curled round my mind or rather my nerves and I could have joined them as I've never been able to join a western religious ceremony. At the end of their acclaiming & triumphant song they cut a coconut in half, giving half to the God & cutting the other portion into little slices, one each for the worshippers, and then, to my delight, a piece for Gush & I. So we celebrated holy communion before the God of Good Fortune.

I'm writing in a little Dak Bungalow near our camp. It's clean & spacious, whitewashed & cool. The moon is sliding down the trellis, the red gravel pathway white. A beast barking in the jungle, a train going past far away among the trees. Like the simple scrubbed room in France that belonged to us long ago & that we never found. You will come again, won't you? Maybe I'll be away longer than you will. Even then –?

Somehow I can't write, Frieda. I want you to know I love you in as many ways as I have moods & failings, and that I cannot come to you is in consonance with everything I've lived. I've never found an easy way & would be scornful if it were. I want a letter from you when I go back to the battalion. I haven't had any mail for a fortnight. Look after your dear body and your baby. Bear him well, Gilly's little brother. I have strange thoughts about him. He means many things to me. Oh many many things there are no words for.

I doubt whether there'll be time for you to send me your vitamin powders – they *were* nice too! – but I've got the golden ring, my talisman. It glitters in the sun in the jungle pools when I strip and dive in & swim. It's a sweet ring and I'm always aware of it. I hope it'll be Highfield next time, Frieda. I love Highfield.

Goodnight, darling,
This love, this pride,
x x x
x x
x x x
Alun

Frieda,

This out of a mixed mood. Writing to you for the first time with your ring on my little finger, for the first time on Xmas Eve, such a macabre Xmas Eve, in the first time of aloneness I've wrung from the absurd season. It's after eleven & the little bandy padre of the Presbyterians has started a carol service in the canteen & the lads are singing Hark the herald angels to his squeezebox. Down the slope across the road the C. of E. padre is ringing a bell in the darkness calling the communicants to midnight mystery. I hear both. I also hear the drunkards in the Mess, the noisy boring choruses that make a bawdy song even out of a carol: and I've spent the afternoon as a steward at the Swimming Gala & the evening as an MC at the Whist Drive & cashier at the Tombola Game. I've always wondered who got the score cards typed out for whist drives & enough packs of cards to go round. And I find it's me. It's a very peculiar discovery. The canteen has been crammed all night with whist & tombola, the floor filthy with cigarettes & papers; & the little padre evokes God & the loved ones at home and I desist. I feel sorry that I must be neutral – isn't it a sin against the Holy Ghost? – to be neutral? – but I do *not* adore him when I bellow 'O Come let us adore him' & I get no spiritual ease at all but a perpetual self castigation so I perhaps am right to go my own way.

Xmas in a mixed mood. I couldn't bear the drunkards in the mess. They're so very boring & unimportant insignificant indifferent – all the negative virtues. And I'm furious with myself, really I'm furious. The doors had opened and I thought I might come & stay with you after Xmas: why not? Officially one can apply for leave up to the 14th of January – and I shut the door of the cage: trap: I'm very cross with the tedious dustcovers I keep pulling over myself.

Gweno has rebuked me gently & powerfully for a particularly bad spate of pessimism round the time I was malingering in hospital and her letters this week have glowed with the marsh light of courageous gaiety. The rival carol singers in the rival services are at it now. Jack Gush gave me two letters to 'deliver' to him tomorrow morning – from his wife. I've kept your parcel unopened & shall break the seals upon the linen tomorrow. Gweno, Frieda. And love that cannot & will not submit to any of us. How I scorn my weakness: and pity it also. And the weakness is that I know fear. Fear of two great wonders uniting in a third which is not me but infinitely more than me.

Frieda, it doesn't matter who is more than who, does it? It's as irrelevant as to ask Are you more than Gilly or less than Gilly? Am I less than thee by overmuch? Have I lost at least for a long time the virtue of the poet? I don't wait for the answer. I feel the humility from which the answer grows, but I ignore the answer. Je pense, donc je suis. Descartes thought: that was all he was sure of. O come ye to Bethlehem. The childish mentality of General Booth saying the devil has all the best tunes. But what has happened is us. I can hardly believe in it: it is as miraculous as God or the nativity. It will go on happening again, God knows when. I can hardly bear to imagine it. It *did* happen, darling, it *did* happen. It was thus & thus, beyond speaking. Would it were now & tonight & tomorrow & tomorrow night. If you would come on leave with me again.

Xmas is a sort of hysteria. I'm going to sleep. Tomorrow I *must* find a little while to myself, to Gweno, Mother, Mair, Frieda. But now it's the weight of my head I must rest away while the steadfast carol & have midnight mass. Frieda, to be away from this hysteria of congregations. To be alone with you, overlooking a cool bay, at an open window, in a deep night, holy, body unto body & the peace of that.

Goodnight darling. No Merry Xmas I wish you, though you are

welcome to it & in duty bound to it as me. I wish you – that you, and that me that is, its own justification & its own eternity.

But darling I am very small. And I am going to sleep.

Goodnight Frieda Buttery, my love.

Boxing Day

Yesterday I didn't find a little while & I've already got to think hard to remember what happened on Xmas Day 1943. There was a service in the morning to which I went & sang some carols and for about the duration of a dream felt a deep pang of gentleness when the associations of the First Nowell overcame me. But that had to stop and after that I watched a football match & then served out dinners: the cooks who had been up all night slaughtering the poultry from their temporary chicken run – all save one cockerel who crowed in triumph all last night. And to every man a bottle of beer, a banana an orange a cigar a packet of sweets – sounds like TS Eliot describing Hannibal's victory march!

I worked out concert programmes all afternoon, ate a huge turkey dinner at 8 & then tried to organise a drunken carol & popular song hour in the canteen. And then, carefully avoiding the drinking party I went to bed & slept till long after Sunday breakfast. And now I'm collecting frocks & slacks & blazers & hats & cigars & drums for tonight's concert. And I hope to write to Dick & to mother some time or other.

I hope you've all had a more becoming and civilised rest. I would dearly love to be with you, but I'm not going to ask for leave because it's too much an escape & I should probe the void here instead because it's the void of the greater part of mankind.

And I've left till the end to tell you that when I woke yesterday morning I cut the calico & wax round my Xmas box from Frieda and with very delicate eyes & fingers considered & explored & was unbearably touched by the box and the blue eyes & the love knot and the pencil & the cocktail shaker* and the chocolates and blades. Bless you for such a sweet potpourri Frieda: you're very dear: & that you made it yourself: I wish I did things instead of dashing in on an odd wave & buying something & never patiently constructing it like a good craftsman putting his love into his gift. But one day I'll become serene. Then I'll make something out of tranquillity.

Thank Gilly for her love & her Xmas Card & give my love to the sea & the little child.

A happy new year to you

Ever your
Alun

I'm sorry about this leave business: Can I come to Coonoor in March perhaps? It's all very vague though, like the future.

---

* Freda's note: *A whiskey whisk* [i.e. a swizzle-stick]

Frieda

I wrote the address & your name last night, in camp, 200 miles away from here. 'Here' is a field, a cactus hedge, new year's eve, nowhere. There's an Indian state town a couple of miles off & we, having arrived here at dusk & fatted ourselves on bully beef & mashed potatoes, went into the town to buy eggs for breakfast & stayed to see Bette Davis in *The Little Foxes*. And now I'm lying under a wavy low mosquito net, pretty uncomfortable & abominably sleepy, having started the journey at 3 a.m. this morning and ridden a motor bike along kucha roads all the way.

And the new year is yours, Frieda, as far as my wishes can give it to you. Which is not far. What do I wish you? Just this 'Be Yourself'. What else? Only the fire in my mind that you lit. If I were to let it go out – how terrible it would be. If it were never to flare up in another Bombay, how much lost? Let there be an again, New Year. Save us.

I wrote you such a morose letter at Xmas. I'm sorry for being so pusillanimous. In the event I turned out to be a little better than my letter. Thinking over the concert I produced, I realise with some joy that it contained a lot of serious criticism veiled in buffoonery and mirth; and that its laughter was clean and either from the mind or the guts, never from the differences between one sexual organ and another. It was an uproarious gregarious concert in the end. I told you I was fetching eight ladies from Poona out to dance & sing in the entr'actes. It was enormous fun. They were a very mixed bag: no intellect, tremendous gusto, an innocent girl of 12 and a hardened soldier's wife of 35: Eurasian girls at their prime of floral development or 'English' girls born out here & never once home & yet solidly English in speech and predilection. It became ultimately an invitation to irresponsible pleasures. I find occasional irresponsibility almost a necessity nowadays – as a kind of laxative – no, as a necessary relief from the unending burden of earth – but not that kind of dissipation. I keep on thinking of those soubrettes – to them every evening is routine, to their hosts (every evening different hosts) each evening is an occasion. What a fate, to make your routine commensurate with the other's 'occasion' – and they had enough pure loving gusto to set all our mess on its mettle & make it feel as if a Pentecostal wind had blown. It was an odd climax to my tedious worries about properties, fatigue parties, footlights, piano tuning & god knows what that go to make a concert or a Xmas. I'd have loved you to see it.

Oh Frieda, goodnight darling. Speaking is too loud tonight – let me seek you & find you in the peaceful forests of sleep. Tyger Tyger.

Je n'oublie que moi même, mais jamais moi et toi,

À jamais
Alun

Jan 1st [1944]: Now a luxury. Alone. In an orchard, with a hurricane lamp under a mangrove tree: a glass of wine, a loaf of bread – and thou. The wine being a double Seagrams, the bread what all troops call

an egg banjo, a fried egg in a tea bun, sold in thousands by canteen walas. And thou. Oh! *you're* not a prosaic substitute. Nor is the wilderness.

The others have all gone off to Cinema or club and I am saved having to go with them because I'm orderly officer. Otherwise courtesy would have insisted on a communal evening in the Club. Jack Gush has just gone in after stuffing an egg banjo & a cup of chah. And we conclude our three day journey tomorrow. Today was infuriating. I had three punctures in my back wheel and was either cursing among a litter of bolts & nuts & spanners & vulcanised patches or roaring through dust clouds at forty to catch the convoy up. You can't write poetry and ride a motor cycle.

The state town was amusing. Gush & I went in on the bike and roared past the Residency (Tudor style) through the gates of the Palace (Victorian Gothic) and pulled up outside the prince's zoo for Gush to exercise his new Zeiss camera. I couldn't think of the names of any of the animals and they were all strange anonymous beasts of God's clown-mind 'We'll have one with a head like this

[*drawing of a head*]

And a neck like this

[*drawing of a neck*]

And what do you think of a chassis something like this

[*drawing of a body*]

Legs? Oh any four legs will do: take those two there

[*drawing*]

And those two:

[*drawing*]

That's fine. Market it.'

We were thrilled with the chorus girl uniforms of the Palace Guard – Merry Widow, école/atelier de – and the huge black bear that was being exercised by a chowkeydar of military age & category A1. *Little Foxes* is a fine macabre film, deliciously pessimistic. [. . .] I liked it. When we came out of what they all agreed was a bloody awful film a little boy of about six came up & said 'Soo-sine sahib,' brandishing a brush & polish: & when we said No, he said 'Jig jig sahib, ek rupee' & pointed to a dark house opposite the cinema. Which is the way our boys get V.D., I suppose. It's just too easy.

I went through all my letters before we left camp, & I put all yours into a bundle and I have them with me. I intended burning them but I couldn't. I hope against hope to get a week's leave in early

Zeiss camera, I couldn't think of the
names of any of the animals and they
were all strange anonymous beasts
of god's clown-mind (" We'll have
one with a head like this

and a neck like this
and what do you think of a chassis
something after this

legs? Oh any four legs will do, take
those two there . and these two
That'll fine. Marker it.

We were thrilled with the chorus
girl uniforms of the Palace Guard
— Merry Widow, écoleide — and
the huge black bear that was
atelier
being exercised by a chowraydar of military
age & category A1. Little Foxes is a fine
macabre film, deliciously pessimistic.

March: *please* let me come & stay with you: may I give them to you then? It's not that I'm afraid of burning you: but I couldn't burn a book of poems I love, I'd have to give it away.

I've been living on a couple of cylinders for a long time: & aware of it, which is some exculpation: but it's very boring to know that you can't go into the locked rooms. Frieda's room was locked, and Alun's, and the new room & the old room and the everlasting room: the only open rooms were the Drill Hall & Madame Tussaud's. And I couldn't look from the window onto Colaba bay & the people on the esplanade. Nor share the innocence and boundlessness of the fore-dawn with the cool sea wind laving our bodies and a nearness that made the world a heaven. I'm afraid of the fighting when it comes. I'll loathe it so utterly, & be so faithless to Life, beloved Life. It is spoiling me already. Yet I refused the chance to escape it. I half think I want it to happen to me to activate the submerged instinct of humanity in me. I'll fight much better for peace than I ever can for war. I'll write better, too. When it at last comes my slow way. My little brother Huw is home from Burma & spending Xmas with Auntie Connie in Darjeeling. She hasn't written to me since her heartbroken letter in August: nothing at Xmas at all. Huw'll help her, she'll be terribly thrilled to have him. He'll talk her head off by evening each day & then he'll dash out like a tomcat in search of what the night has to offer. Glyn, my other brother, is in our division now & is coming down to the jungle to train with us. He was hoping to get leave, but I believe it's been postponed for him too. He asked if he might write to you. I told him you were in Tuticorin & that later you'd be engrossed with baby. I didn't think you could do with a guest. Yet I can't help asking you, selfishly, that I may come. I'd be very quiet and not a bit temperamental. I'd sit on the lawn for hours & not want anything. You wouldn't be self conscious, Frieda, would you? I mean we both would be a little, but it would cancel out. Are you well?

What did you 'hear' that made you send me the ring I wear and am so fond of? The day broke so slowly yesterday, it was perishing cold, the coldness wrung & withered my mind & I kept saying How long will the day be? How long? And when at last the sun touched me with warm hands something childish in me crooned like a pigeon. Do we ever get much farther than that little cycle of nay & yea?

Thank you for the poem of the journey, the man sousing his buffal*ow!* And the life he does not know within the movement. You'll be weary of me saying 'shorten it by half' – it's a ruthless thing to keep saying – But, darling, your poem is complete at the end of the swiftly flowing silent stream. Your god of good beginnings should come in there. And leave the end to him. He will refashion it. It's lovely the first two stanzas.

What do you mean 'being of use to me?' You came that there should be more life: *and* you sent me razor blades also.

Goodnight, Frieda: sois patiente.

Love Alun

Frieda Dearest,
Your letter from Nagercoil was a long time reaching me. Today your Highfield letter came too. So I'm writing to both of them. Bless you & bless Gilly for surviving what happened. Thank God it was as brief as it was horrible:* No, Frieda, I've not been subjected to the stress of such a dread, and I don't know, I don't know. I swerve & wobble in my 'soul' (?) so much under the steady strain of this tightrope war, although I've only known it's normal behind the lines humdrum, I feel ashamed of my waverings when I know what other harder dreads are imposed on you or sometimes one, sometimes another of those who have meaning to me. I can't say anything Frieda, – it only increases my love for you & Gilly to feel the hazard you were in. Love responds more vitally to danger than to any other stimulus, I think. Or it goes to earth, afraid to be real & to grapple. I know there's a shyness in all my loving, the kind of shyness that you throw round something you're afraid of chancing in the rough & tumble. But you say the baby hasn't known about all this, and now it's over, is more with you than before. Sweet sweet sweet baby, bless his head. I won't come & see you till he's born now, Frieda, – Victor Odling was quite quite wrong, but don't correct him, it's nobody's business to know anything just now. But I will come, somehow, I will, will, will.

Why should I have to? So many gestures to be made, so many difficulties to be made, so many renunciations, so much patience. Within the patience impatience, within the fortitude weakness.

---

* It seemed that Gilly's nanny had V.D.

Why are people ashamed or afraid of weakness, their own weakness, their human honest native weakness? Oh weary game. I want to write so badly: yet I don't want to perfectly: it isn't clear in me (yet often at the beginning it isn't clear – it's simply strong: perhaps it isn't strong enough in me yet). Yet I'm unwilling to write when I don't know next week, when I expect the cataclysm and have a stubborn feeling that when that has happened values will be different & the old no longer valid. Now tonight there's a boozing party in the mess to celebrate an ancient wound of the Regiment – Rourke's Drift in the Zulu War of 1879 – and I don't want to drink, yet I should go. I could start this story: but would it begin aright? Should I start it objectively, writing it from the outside, disciplining it? Or shall I let it rush over the weir? It's bad for a writer to feel emotional – he floods & corrupts his sentences & themes with his own emotions. That's old & true: yet so unfair. Why should intense feeling discolour a story? A poem can hold the wild liquid: I'm afraid to start this story. Also I'm afraid of the nothing that will be left if I finish it. I've finished so many things these last days, it's got me down. I've packed all my kit, & sorted out my papers, revised my poems & sent them off to Allen & Unwin, – burnt all your letters, darling, oh with such trembling & gentle but fierce sorrow, made arrangements for my accumulated raw pees* to go to Gweno: I've made everything so tidy. And it shouldn't be tidy like that – it should sprawl along healthily and confidently into the future: not detach itself from the future so neatly and circumspectly. I couldn't bring myself to send you my sports jacket & flannels: perhaps I will yet: but I couldn't think of them getting to Highfield & you airing them & hanging them up for a long time. I've crammed them into my broken cabin trunk & put a number & lots of mysterious colour paints on it. There, it's done.

* rupees

I've been lucky to get my poems back in peace. They came by sea mail together with Robert Graves's detailed criticism & comments on them. I spent three nights working at them, not very much, not as much as they needed. But time was in a hurry & I had to be shot of them. All in all, I think it's a better book than *Raiders' Dawn* – more objective and the words have more balance. Maybe not as 'poetic' though. I've included 'Wood Song', 'Peasant Song', 'Ways', and 'The Way Back'. May I, Frieda? You are willing to *be* in the book, aren't you darling? Please.

I've called the book HA HA AMONG THE TRUMPETS (Job 39). Please get a Bible & read the beautiful chapter it is. The wild ass – who has given him freedom that he heeds not the call of the mule driver? The ostrich who leaves her eggs in the warm sand & has no love & no satisfaction. The battle charger who smelleth afar off the shouting of the captains and the din of battle. Lovely lovely words. God is speaking them, the bible says. But I don't think he is. I think it's a man is speaking them, with an understanding of beauty & a longing in him. I'm blind to God, I can't see him at all. My mind is clenched & he isn't there at all, my mind is like a clenched fist. It won't open. Nor will it strike, either. I'm not going to write this story. I'm sad about that. I want to be less I, but I can't lose myself in anything else not here, not now, not yet.

Dick is coming on Friday night, I hope. Poona is quite near but it's been put out of bounds to us & I may have considerable difficulty in getting in. I'll get in though. Or I'll fetch him out here. Of course I'll see him. I had a long letter from him today. He's a bit 'digalon', unhappy that is. He's got the same strain on him as we have. He's got more responsibility that I have: I've discovered that too little responsibility distresses me infinitely more than too much. I hope I can spend Sunday night at Poona Hotel with Dick, & Sunday morning. Then he goes all the way to Highfield, his letter says. Gweno said in one letter 'You don't understand how difficult is it for us even to *breathe* sometimes'. I'm like that too.

We had a day by the sea last week. It was fine: there were chalets in the palm groves all up the beach. We could be there. It was alright for us. I could be *so* happy. We could be.

I lay in the sand & let the tide come right up slowly & deposit a lick of surf, dirty brown spume, on my body. Reluctant to be anything else but that sun & sea. I saw a film last night – *Stage Coach* – the wild west is very like India, parts of Belgaum & Kohlapur – arid, rocky, animist, the rocks monoliths are master of it all, surviving & conquering the barrenness. It (was) *is* fine, this sterile unbending monolithic country.

I want to stop writing and to rest by your side in your arms. I want that very badly, it's made me sigh. The poems will be out in the Autumn: I've asked Gweno to send you a copy: so you've got one Xmas present being made ready for next year. But I can't look at the future – I can't see any distance at all. Oh well, the time I've wasted, dreadful.

Will you give my dearest love to Gillian, very specially please.

And for yourself, Know I am conscious all the time that a whole life is being thrown away all the time we are denying & are denied each other. That other life haunts me inescapably – & I desire it ineluctably. It makes the rest of living sad.

Dick will bring some books I have. And some news. But not *this* love. Only just love Dick will bring, lighthearted love, good luck love.

I'll write quickly again.

Goodnight darling

I watched the words fade from your letters, each one as I burnt them. They grew nearer & nearer to me all the time. The ashes were delicate & intangible. The wind blew them about.

x x x x x x   Alun

217

I'm enclosing Robert Graves's
comments on the poems. Will
you keep them for me? I'll
come & see you in June: July.
Promise.

214565 *Lt. A. Lewis*
6th Bn South Wales Borderers
ABPO 21

Sunday [30 January]

Frieda dearest,
Evening already, the chatter of sunset, the coppersmith, red flowers, crows on the flagstaff, Dick in his shirt sleeves, me in my trousers letting my pimply shoulders cool after a tepid bath given gratis by Dick's pomaded Muslim. Everything seems in order, doesn't it?

I've never been gladder of a thing happening than this of Dick's coming. I wouldn't have had him leave you so abruptly, nor have the power or wish to draw him this far from you. I wasn't asking anything of anybody, of you, of Gweno, of Dick. I wasn't transmitting, I was a dead station, off the air. And then Dick rang me up at lunch time on Saturday from Poona and something in the crawling sucking squelching morass of my nerves began tinkling, faintly & distantly. Half an hour later I'd obtained leave from the C.O., found a truck, told Tudor to pack some pyjamas for me, and I began singing. For the first time for weeks & weeks. I know you'd send Dick if there was need. I can talk a little about need now – it's the underlining of my silence for the past fortnight, and I don't think I'm able to say much more than that now. Anyway I found myself articulate last night & I told Dick what was wrong with me. And today the strain is less, though its nature is to come & go.

Frieda, I can't write to you. You know the aloneness and the seemingly impotent and closed-in love that is outside the perimeter of the aloneness. It's almost more than I can get my pen to write to say that I think all the time of you & baby and will strive to be near you the farther away I go. And of you & Gilly and some gentle impulse is always smoothing your hair & her hair with a hand softer than mine but me. And other things I can't say at all.

Please, on future letters, put *If undelivered return to F.A., Highfield etc.* Will you, dear? Lest they go the weary round of effects to be disposed of and break a heart in the end.

I'll write to you lots of times once this tension is eased off me.

Give these special kisses to you & Gilly

x x x x x x x x

The tattooed arm.

xx Ever,

Alun

214565 Lt. A. Lewis
6th Bn. South Wales Borderers
c/o ABPO 21

Feb 10th Thursday

Frieda dearest,

I've been very silly and troubled these last few weeks and I've never been able to write to you. Dick brought you inside the stony laager and we made a fire of branches over the weekend and sat by it warm and quick. The strangeness, the distance, the going away, the torments I inflict on myself and the desolation that enervates and exhausts all moved back one pace, two paces, three paces and I could look without dropping my eyes. And now I'm in the impersonal, imperturbable mood which comes after a danger or an evil experience, when there is no clear emotion or sense of peril or failure or escape, but just an insulated quietness from which one acts and considers & waits. I don't mind what happens now: I've got myself in rein, I think I'll be what I am expected to be & do what I ought to do and that in itself is a scriptural simplicity. For the rest, I feel that it's out of my hands now: and I feel no distress at having to go unresolved as it were, leaving many majestic worlds scarcely known and the depth of the sea unsounded. I know Life won't stay still: while I'm away you will be happening and perhaps the solution will be coming nearer: but some deep wisdom tells me Let it be in itself. And the accent is so heavily upon work and duty that I can let it be more easily. Something nearly died in me last week: I was horrified with the sense of loss and vainness. But it didn't quite die.

I'm much too introvert and querulous, aren't I? I've got so used to looking inside myself for poems and stray thoughts; I can't get out of the habit: I ought to be mixing and yapping and getting to know things: well, I can't, & that's that. And although my job is worse done because I plan inwardly & not objectively I still can't help it. I think it was a shrewd assessment of myself, not humility that compelled me to refuse that Intelligence Corps job last September. I've still got to prove myself satisfactorily. Maybe I will this time. I've finished with the fear & loathing and failure of it, I hope, & my nerves have stopped spinning & getting dizzy & wearying my body with the insistent fretting of the guilty & trivial in the mind. I'm steady again, & can sing welsh songs without trouble.

And you, Frieda? I've got your letter here, the one when Dick was with you. I'm sorry there was that hiatus between you & Dick. But don't you do him a little wrong? He's a lion of sympathy, you know, great firm paws he has, and a wide slow care & balance. He's not volatile & mercurial, nor does he leap intuitively to understanding. He'll maybe puzzle you out for days. But he's wonderfully clean & methodical in his thought, and he knows a thing before knowing has become something he can use. But he wasn't sad about you & Gilly: he came to Poona with a world of life in him & he'd mastered all the burden of his soldiering which had depressed him a lot only a fortnight before when he wrote me a very distracted letter.

You talk again of 'belonging', Frieda. I don't know what it is – it's too simple a relationship for my waywardness. As far as I know myself, I can either be positively alive and in love, or I can be negative, an element as unresisting as air, through which people can walk, or a book that people can open, read, throw away, burn – this collapse of self & the painfully fortified values is something which prevents me from ever saying certainly 'I belong' – for worthlessness belongs to no one. And when I have the marvellous feeling of I am I, then I can identify myself with whatever is beautiful and adorable and perennial in world and thee, and I can suffer whatever is dreadful and shameful & sorrowing. 'I know you & I can't be fulfilled', you say. Yet your poem is saying louder than all the angels that we *were* fulfilled as soon as we met. Your lovely poem takes me into green pastures more surely that the passage of all things that decay: and as long as that first flash of the sword is true there is always a truth in us. And truth *is* fulfilment. What other end can there be to desire but the truth that was in the beginning – ?

Do I weary you with my difference from you? I know we are thinking & feeling differently to each other now: but that was always in our natures. And it's also in our destiny. Oh the *thrill* of myself to thyself, sweet swordsman, the dancer & the dance, the wind & the cry of the wind, & the child making its way into the world through you; & Gilly in the world wondering and knowing; and the hazards between & the long cycles of returning to the revelation and the incarnation. There is no end to all this, except the accidental end, the bulb fusing, the mind failing, the body ceasing to function, lungs & heart & eyes. Don't be fretted with loss, Frieda; I feel wonderfully happy whenever the certainty moves in me that I have lived indestructibly in thee. And in mother, & Mair, and boyhood, and Gweno, and words sometimes joining in flame. So I try not to shiver when a cold gout strikes me & I feel a collapse in the nervous clocktower of my being.

I won't write a long letter about having a swim with Dick or seeing *Now Voyager* with Dick, or trying to phone you with Dick. I don't want to say the lake is beautiful & remote, I swam in it this evening remotely & boyishly. Nor that I'm glad with all my heart I've finished with waiting & shilly shally (though I've no expectations). I've had enough of a life of routine & soccer matches in the evening! I'm glad enough, just for myself.

For you I wanted to come & see you first, but it will be very wonderful to come in the end. Don't worry over the hairs on my head. May you not be tried harder than you can bear. And I'll surely come up through the trees to the lawn to the splendour & the homecoming & the child & Gilly & us.

Ever,

Alun

3909998 QMS Thomas,
British Inf Sub-Sec,
G.H.Q (I) 2nd Echelon,
Jhansi, U.P., India.

25th March 1944.

Dear Mrs. Aykroyd,

I am at a loss to begin this message of sad news which you may have already heard but the fact of the matter is that Lieut Alun Lewis, serving with The South Wales Borderers, asked me to let you know should anything happen to him, so it is my painful duty, in obedience to his request, to inform you of Lieut Lewis' accidental death from a revolver shot on the 5th March.

I had known Mr. Lewis for over two years, from the time he joined our Battalion in Suffolk, and we were the best friends – I believe he spent his leave with you last August.

I have read many of his poems and stories and I think it was very fitting that the B.B.C. in their Radio Newsreel Programme a week last Thursday, should have paid him a last tribute by reading one of his poems. Perhaps you heard it yourself.

I feel sure you will join me in expressing the deepest sympathy to his wife and family. One of his brothers is with the R.A.F. in India and I have written to him with the tragic news.

    Yours sincerely

    S. Thomas

Dear Mrs. Akroyd,

Thank you very much for your kind and understanding letter. You have caught Alun's spirit and outlook and your words have been a great source of comfort to me.

There is no need for me to say anything to you about the extent of our loss and sorrow for you know and understand. Huw says 'Alun was more than a brother to me; he was a way of life.' And that is how we all feel. My only comfort is the thought that he didn't fall into Japanese hands and that it was clean and quick; that he had no painful foreknowledge and that he didn't suffer at all. I like to think that a kindly Providence intervened to save him from worse.

But what a waste it all is! I can only beg you young parents who are left to carry on, to build better than we did so that this can never happen again. Then, perhaps, all this agony and suffering won't have been wholly in vain.

Gweno is very brave but she looks worn and tired. She is the most precious thing he has left us and we shall love and cherish her dearly always. I know his last message to me would have been 'Take care of Gweno & Mair'. Strangely, this was the last sentence in his last letter to us written on Feb. 8th. I am so perplexed about so many things that seem to have stirred you too, that I wish I could talk to you. Sometimes I think that both he and I had some foreknowledge. I don't know and I am very troubled. All I can do is to try my best to show his friendly kind spirit wherever I go until my dying day.

And now let me wish you and the new life that Gillian is waiting as anxiously to welcome, a safe and easy journey. Perhaps you will let me know when all is normal and you are up and about again?

And my very grateful thanks to you and Mr. Akroyd for all your kindness to the son who is so dear to me. My best wishes to you all.

Gwladys E. Lewis